I0820074

FOUNDATIONS

PICASSO SCULPTURE

FOUNDATIONS

TIMELESS DESIGN THAT FEELS PERSONAL

NATE BERKUS

with HEATHER SUMMERVILLE

Simon Element

New York Amsterdam/Antwerp London Toronto Sydney/Melbourne New Delhi

To Jeremiah, I would not recognize this world without your love and everything you do for us, every day. To all of our "moments in between," you are the definition of love and support.

Poppy and Oskar, you both have redefined the meaning of home for me, and I am so lucky to be your dad. I could not love you more.

To my mother, Nancy Golden, who taught me to love shopping and transformation.

CONTENTS

VANITY FAIR 100 YEARS
CHRISTIAN DIOR
1947–1957
ASSOULINE

LOST NEW YORK
PAUL HAMLYN
NEW YORK
SAVAGE BEAUTY
Nancy Milford
DORIS KEARNS GOODWIN
TEAM OF RIVALS
THE POLITICAL GENIUS OF ABRAHAM LINCOLN
WALTER CRONKITE
A REPORTER'S LIFE
ANDREW CARNEGIE
DAVID NASAW
WILL YOU MISS ME WHEN I'M GONE?
KATHARINE GRAHAM
PERSONAL HISTORY
John Adams.
DAVID McCULLOUGH
JOE DIMAGGIO
RICHARD BEN CRAMER

INTRODUCTION

Thirty years in . . .

It doesn't *feel* like three decades have passed since I printed my first business cards in Chicago. It was 1995 and I had some hope, youthful self-confidence, and just enough fear. Thirty years is a long time to do what I do. As this anniversary neared, I kept circling back to all I've learned and tried along the way. The mistakes I've made and what I did to overcome them.

As different as my life looks now—I have grown my firm to forty people and my family to four—the pull I feel toward design and architecture that represents the people who live with it, and my appreciation for things that stand the test of time still remain the foundation of my design process.

This is the book I have always wanted to write, but it wasn't until now that I could. I needed the years of designing and thinking, of working through each project, of learning something every day.

I believe your home should tell your story. I've said this from the beginning. But what does that *actually mean*? How do you put it into practice? What makes a room *feel* authentic to the people who live there? These were the questions I was considering when thinking about where to take you with this book.

Truly good design does not expire. It is never about the new or the latest. It is honest, emotional, something you see with your eyes but feel with your heart. I remember an enthusiastic salesperson who followed me through two miles of the Kitchen & Bath Show in Las Vegas, hoping to impress me with his touch-activated, color-changing countertops. All I could think was, "I'm never using those."

EIGHT EUROPEAN ARTISTS

When I need inspiration, I look in two directions: up and backwards. Up to the homes and rooms and estates that are maybe way too grand for a particular project but are always filled with incredible ideas. (You may not be able to live in a seventeenth-century Italian villa, but you could re-create the floors in your entry.) I look backwards to the past for historic references I can interpret or use in a modern way. I will show you how to do both in this book.

I am passing on my entire experience to you, so you can start to think about decorating in a very personal way, to see design through a new lens that brings your own creative vision into focus. What is it that is important and interesting to you? Let's figure that out first—and then let's be thoughtful about the spaces, objects, and furniture we surround ourselves with.

In our rush to "finish" a room, it is easy to feel pressure to make decisions too fast. Those chairs. That lamp. This paint color. Just get it done. But let me ask you this: Why are you rushing? Decorating is meant to be enjoyable, and rooms are meant to come together over time. Some of the spaces in this book took years to assemble, piece by piece. Personal design is never instantaneous. Give yourself permission to take the time you need to make a space that you will love living in.

My greatest hope is that this book gives you the confidence to find and hear your own voice with clarity, to shut out the noise from social media, magazines, catalogs, and the design industry, myself included.

Are you ready? Then let's go make some brave design choices—together.

LOEWE

1

MAKE IT PERSONAL

2

EMBRACE HISTORY

3

INTRODUCE CHARACTER

4

DEVELOP YOUR VISION

PART 1

THE FOUR TENETS OF GOOD DESIGN

I have spent the last three decades walking through front doors that don't belong to me. Often for the purpose of reimagining what lies beyond, sometimes just to visit. I have come to understand that what matters most in a home is a sense of connection, a deep link to the space, what has taken place there—or will—and the objects inside. Without this, a room can be beautiful, but it can also feel impersonal. I have been in expensive homes full of expensive things, that somehow still felt empty. The rooms said nothing. Where had the people who live there come from? What did they do for joy? What moments did they celebrate together as a family? Everything was too perfect, and I have always felt that the cracks are "how the light gets in," to borrow a lyric from Leonard Cohen.

Connection in a space is an abstract notion. How you achieve it can come about organically. For a room to be successful—and by that, I mean a room that feels like a reflection of you and works for how you live your life—it needs to be personal *and* have history, character, and a developed vision. My Four Tenets of Good Design are not rules to follow, as much as they are a framework to help you think about design, not just as something pretty to look at but as something that inspires you to be the best version of yourself in the moments when no one is watching.

You can see each of the four tenets in the parlor level of our former NYC townhouse. The pottery bird on the mantel was brought back from Peru, where Jeremiah and I got engaged—something personal. The furniture is a mix of nineteenth-century French antiques and vintage pieces from the 1930s and 1960s—a little history. The space includes a Louis XVI–style fireplace, deep crown moulding, and light oak floors in a classic chevron pattern—the character. And the vision, how it all came together, was tied to the room's purpose: introducing guests, in a thoughtfully edited way, to the aesthetic style of the rest of the home.

1 MAKE IT PERSONAL

I've always believed in the power of *things*.

I've always believed in the power of *things*.

There is both alchemy and magic in their ability to transport us—to a place, a time, a loved one, a memory. If the objects you choose to live with do not tell the story of you, if they do not help you move through your space with a sense of joy and familiarity, then, you haven't yet arrived where I'm hoping to take you now. Even though it may look beautiful, what you've created is not really your home but more like a showroom, a copy of someone else's ideas.

A favorite book displayed prominently on your coffee table. Artwork that represents all the places you've called home. A collection of antique silver frames started by your grandmother, continued by you. These pieces say more about you, as a person, than most of the other design decisions you will make.

Every designer has their own process. For me, creating a home starts with getting to know my clients—at times better than they know themselves. Their willingness to open up is the price of having a home that reflects them. That level of introspection doesn't come from scrolling through their Pinterest board or Instagram feed. It doesn't happen after one or two (or even ten) meetings to look at pages pulled from a magazine. That is mainly just noise. It doesn't tell me enough about who they are and what they want to see mirrored back at them in their space.

I have a sociological approach to decorating. I want to know what someone's favorite book is and why. Their favorite thing to make in the kitchen and how they serve it. Does everybody pile up around the island, or do they sit at a beautifully set table? With these answers, I can make decisions about seating, storage, floorplans, even whether the serving dishes are kept on display.

As this chapter unfolds, I will be asking you to open up. To turn inward, instead of outward for inspiration. To ask yourself the questions that really matter, and to be honest in your answers—to quiet the noise. I want you to create a home truly tailored to you, one that speaks to who you are, where you came from, and the beautiful and meaningful life you aspire to live.

PREVIOUS PAGE: Establishing a room's purpose is another way to create a personal connection with your space. The open furniture arrangement in our NYC dining room, the way the table is set to one side, was intentional. We wanted to make a lot of memories there; the extra room allowed us to welcome as many friends and family as possible.

ABOVE: This striped fabric bookmark is something I bought on a whim in Mexico, because I thought it was handsome. It sits on a book about my friend, the artist James Brown. The carved hands on top are from one of my ten thousand trips to a local antiques mall. You learn so much about me from this one grouping of objects: where I've been, who I love, where I like to shop.

WHERE ARE YOU FROM?

I love the phrase "putting down roots." It speaks not just to our current self but also to the history that we are making, the heritage we are bringing with us into a space . . . *our roots*.

How our past becomes a part of our home can look and feel many different ways. Maybe you've inherited your great-grandmother's "good" dishes and need a way to display them. Maybe reconnecting with your Mexican heritage means covering your favorite armchair with a colorful Otomi fabric or setting the table with hand-embroidered placemats.

Finding meaningful ways to include these types of objects in your home's story is always energy well spent. They are not just a representation of where you come from but a connection to your memories of that place. My goal in designing a space is always to remind people of the best times of their lives. When the world outside feels overwhelming, these gestures inside—the ones that remind us of our own stories and history—can help keep us balanced.

---

1. South American pottery candleholders that belonged to my late partner, Fernando Bengoechea.
2. Hand-painted lebrillo dinner plates hung in a sunroom. These are from Mexico, but the original designs date back to fifteenth-century Spain.
3. A nineteenth-century Flemish tapestry on the wall behind a headboard.
4. Vintage Mexican pottery grouped together on a mantel.

1

2

3

4

WHERE HAVE YOU BEEN?

Many years ago, I was renovating my first studio apartment in New York City. It had a tiny kitchen with four upper cabinets and four lower, and I wanted to find interesting hardware for the doors. I searched all over Manhattan for the perfect knobs and pulls. Then, that summer, as I was unskillfully scooting around Patmos, Greece, on vacation, I stopped in the local marine hardware store on an errand, and I spotted some handmade, unlacquered brass latches (designed for boats, not kitchens) and bought eight immediately. For the entire time I lived in that apartment, each morning when I reached for a coffee cup and every night when I put away the plates, I was connected to the memory of summer in Greece with good friends, great food, and surprisingly incredible hardware.

Everywhere I go, I look for the simplest representation of that place—rustic tables and ancient objects from Peru or woven textiles from Laos. Crafts that were made by hand and are a beautiful expression of a place's culture.

Think about the places you've experienced, the destinations beyond your vacation highlight reel. Is there a particular town, village, or street you've seen and felt and loved? A museum you visited that your mind wanders to often? A hotel you return to because it makes you feel like the best version of yourself?

Spend some time visually examining these places. (If you have photos, even better.) Focus on the small details: the patinated finishes, the old door knobs and hinges, the colors, the natural light. Find the moments that resonate with you. Then think about how to bring those elements into your home. Do you need to search your local architectural salvage yard for nineteenth-century knobs? Spend an afternoon at a flea market buying up glazed pottery in muted, matte tones that remind you of the beach? Whatever the reference, make the effort—you will be so happy you did.

PREVIOUS PAGE: Jeremiah and I started collecting small, ceramic bulls, known as Toritos de Pucará, when we lived in Los Angeles. Traditionally, in Peru, these figures are placed on the roof for good luck and to bring prosperity.

LEFT: I brought back this moody photograph, *The Last Ranchero* by Oswaldo Ruiz, from my first trip to Mexico City over twenty years ago. I love the story behind it as much as the image itself, a snapshot of the last man to work on the only remaining plot of land on what was once a huge ranch.

RIGHT: This edited group of furniture and objects represents many of the places that inspire me: The painting is by James Brown, an American artist who was living in Mexico. The lamp is in the style of Alberto Giacometti, an important Swiss artist, who worked mostly in France. It wears a lampshade that was handwoven in Mexico. The chair is Italian modernist. The bench is French from the 1950s.

WHAT DO YOU ALREADY LOVE?

Maybe you're starting your design journey with one piece you really love; maybe you have a room full of them. Take the time to take stock of the things you live with. Which pieces remind you of a special memory? Which ones do you feel reflect you? Which only serve a purpose? Do any do all three?

Knowing which pieces you share a connection with gives me—and the designers at my firm—a starting point. They tell us what we will be designing around, and what you're drawn to. I think often of a particular project, where the homeowner wanted to keep only two items: a single console, one of the few pieces of furniture she ever bought for herself, and a group of vintage glass lanterns that her family had collected together.

That console became the key for this woman's entire vision of her home. It was iron with wood accents, which helped us define her style (something she had never been able to do): slightly industrial, slightly rustic, and slightly imperfect. So we reached for pieces that had patina and a hint of masculinity—no gloss, nothing modern.

Everyone has bought one thing they love for their home. What's yours? It could be an antique chest you saved up for in college, or a pair of chairs with arms that curve perfectly. Take some time to identify these objects and then ask yourself: Why do you love it? What details make it special to you?

The answers will help you understand what you like, and how you want these objects to show up in your home. They can lead you to an Etsy maker who could turn the blouse you love but no longer wear into a handmade lampshade, or to eBay to look for vintage French fabrics that remind you of the pillows your grandmother kept on her bed. This part of the journey—learning about yourself, unearthing treasures, making your world bigger—is the best part.

OPPOSITE: My mom had a tortoise shell that she brought back from Mexico and had preserved. When I was growing up, it hung over our family room fireplace in Minnesota. I wanted to capture that memory in our Los Angeles home.

LEFT: This French Art Deco tambour screen was one of the first pieces of furniture our clients bought together for their new home, so we arranged it in a corner of their living room, where they could see it regularly.

BELOW: The old oil painting hanging in this NYC bathroom represented so many things for the clients. They both love and respect history, and they wanted pieces in their newly renovated home that introduced influences from a different time.

WHAT'S IN YOUR CLOSET?

When I'm visiting a client's home for the first time, they inevitably want to take me straight to the kitchen. I appreciate that because it's where the snacks live, but my favorite first stop when we are starting to discuss design is the closet.

Here's why: If I see rows of floral blouses, I immediately know I'm going to reach for English prints and wallpaper. If there's nothing but preppy staples, I'll do a deep dive into fabrics that feel like men's suiting—herringbones and pinstripes—and lean heavily on accessories. If it's wall-to-wall European minimalism, the colors I suggest are going to be neutral. All of this—the materials, the patterns, the palette, the fabrics—helps me craft an overall direction for the home's style that's going to feel like the client.

Pretend you're visiting your closet for the first time. Step back and look for similarities in colors, patterns, and fabrics. Maybe you never realized you owned so many striped shirts. Or you notice a certain shade of burgundy plays heavily in your accessory lineup. Make a list of everything that catches your eye, from your preferred color of leather shoe to the horn buttons on a coat.

These details are clues that can help you start choosing furniture and fabrics and details for your home. The fact that you have half a dozen belts with aged brass buckles means you're probably going to like a similar finish on your bathroom faucets. Your ivory scarves would play just as well as a soft, highly textured fabric on a chair. Find the patterns and rhythms in your closet, and then search for those keywords. See where it takes you.

LEFT: Jeremiah and I chose a wool runner with a thin pinstripe for the stairs of our NYC townhouse. The pattern reminded me of one of my favorite double-breasted suits.

RIGHT: If you are someone who admires handsome watches or wears beautiful jewelry, consider pulling in warm metal finishes, as we did around this fireplace.

My long-time design partner, Lauren Gordon, loves a stripe. She has a stack of cable-knit sweaters and a lot of green in her wardrobe. Those influences come together in a subtle way here: the texture on the rug, the pinstripe on the chair, the color of the painted cabinets.

Sometimes a limited but strategic use of color—like the vintage Italian sconces used in this LA bedroom—can be more impactful than painting the entire room a bold shade.

ANOTHER THING . . .

Your closet can also help you steer clear of design decisions you may regret later. If you've been eyeing a bright floral armchair but can't seem to bring yourself to follow through with the purchase, take a walk around your closet. Do you see any bright florals? If not, you should question whether this is a trend you'll move away from soon.

WHO DO YOU ASPIRE TO BE AT HOME?

Family dinners are a priority in our home. The things our children say out loud around the table give us a week's worth of laughs. As much as I admire the person who can whip up a three-course meal on a Wednesday night, that's just not a realistic goal for my husband and me. But here's what is: great wine, takeout, and a beautifully set table. We take something low effort and dress it up, make it feel special, which makes us feel like we are winning both at hosting and parenting. This is why we keep a drawer stocked with white candles, and why we're always searching for hand-glazed pottery, woven placemats, embroidered napkins, and good silver to have on hand.

This is how *we* prioritize *our* happiness in *our* home. What would that look like for you? If you want to entertain more, but a kitchen you're not proud of is stopping you, then updating it should be a priority. Maybe you already entertain a lot, but you want the mood to feel more sophisticated. Would something as simple as buying a silver tray from your local antiques market to serve your next charcuterie board on let you step into that aspirational image of yourself?

Figure out the things that are going to make you feel like the best version of yourself. Then consider the investments, large or small, you can make in your home to accommodate them.

IF YOU ASPIRE TO BE SOMEONE WHO . . .

1. **READS MORE,** can you find a quiet corner—preferably near a window—to place a comfortable chaise and a lamp?

2. **SETS A BEAUTIFUL TABLE MORE OFTEN,** can you store your glassware, plates, serving pieces, and favorite candlesticks close to your dining area? Not having to travel between rooms makes setting a lovely table so much faster.

3. **ENTERTAINS AT HOME,** do you have space on your countertop that could be repurposed as a bar area, where guests can congregate and make a cocktail with everything they need?

1

2

3

THE WHAT I LIKE LIST

Hopefully this chapter feels empowering and not too much like work. Everything you've learned about yourself—what you like, what you don't like, what you might like—are the foundations of your design style. How they evolve and take their place in your home comes later as we continue through this book together.

For now, what I want you to take with you is a list of thoughtful, truthful answers to the questions I asked you to consider. Everything on your What I Like List should speak to you in a very personal way. For example, here's mine. It will (and should) look nothing like yours, apart from the format, and that's the point.

WHERE ARE YOU FROM?

I'M FROM California.

WHEN I THINK OF THIS PLACE, I PICTURE light, an ease to living, nature, linen upholstery, potted trees indoors.

MY HERITAGE (OR CULTURAL BACKGROUND) is Jewish, East Coast, and Midwest.

WHEN I THINK OF MY HERITAGE, IT REMINDS ME OF my grandmother's navy and white rooms, Sunday dinners, and a home filled with antique furniture and printed French fabrics.

MY KEY SEARCH WORDS ARE: Antique marble mantels, Italian mid-century lighting, French fabrics, architectural salvage.

WHERE HAVE YOU BEEN?

MY FAVORITE PLACES TO TRAVEL ARE Portugal, Mexico, and Southeast Asia.

WHEN I THINK OF THESE PLACES, I PICTURE things made by hand. Beautifully woven textiles, pottery, plates, and baskets.

THE PLACE WHERE I FEEL THE MOST LIKE MYSELF is in my own home after following my own advice.

WHEN I PICTURE IT, I SEE . . .

YOU WILL ALWAYS FIND ME in a flea market or antiques store because I love both a sense of discovery *and* a great deal.

MY KEY SEARCH TERMS ARE: Local antiques shops and design stores, estate jewelers, flea markets near me.

WHAT DO YOU ALREADY LOVE?

I COULD NEVER PART WITH any of my framed photographs. Our family loves looking at them and remembering past adventures.

I'VE HAD some silver boxes since my first job at an auction house in Chicago in 1995, where I was introduced to decorative arts. Over the years, I have bought thousands of silver boxes to line bookshelves and coffee tables for clients. But when I look at the first pieces I purchased, I remember that boy at the auction house who knew nothing about silver hallmarks and just liked something because it was pretty and well made.

MY KEY SEARCH TERMS ARE: Vintage silver boxes, Japanese bronze figures, vintage leather picture frames.

WHAT'S IN YOUR CLOSET?

I OWN too many sweaters and shoes.

EVERYTHING IN MY CLOSET is shades of camel, ivory, gray, or brown.

MY FAVORITE WINTER COAT IS MADE OF camel hair.

I WEAR A LOT OF T-shirts and crewneck sweaters.

WHEN I'M REALLY DRESSING UP, I WEAR a coat and tie or a leather jacket.

MY KEY SEARCH TERMS ARE: Men's suede, camel, brown.

WHO DO YOU ASPIRE TO BE AT HOME?

I WANT TO BE SOMEONE WHO finds joy in the unexpected. I've spent the last thirty years loving not knowing what I'm going to find around the next corner. When Jeremiah and I first started dating, the trips we took to places neither of us had been before helped reveal ourselves to each other. What one of us (or both) reached for in a flea market in Mexico. What caught my eye versus what caught his at a museum in Madrid.

I CAN DO THAT BY always bringing home or seeking out things that best represent a place or a culture.

I WOULD LOVE TO SPEND MORE TIME with my family discovering new places.

I COULD START MAKING MY HOME MORE INSPIRING BY allowing my husband to execute more of his vision and by being open to change. Jeremiah likes when things have room to breathe. I have a hard time *not* being surrounded by all the things that have meaning to me at the same time.

MY KEY SEARCH TERMS ARE: Silver trays, sterling silver picture frames, handwoven objects.

REALITY CHECK

ARE YOU IN THE RIGHT HOUSE?

Throughout my career, I have asked clients the same questions I asked you to consider in this chapter. I've gathered inspirational imagery with them, searching out what they respond to in terms of architectural styles, historical references, colors, finishes, and so on—a process we'll talk about later in part one.
I have spent hours exploring every inch of their home. Then, I pause and do a reality check-in: Does their inspiration align with the home they live in? Sometimes it doesn't.

The truth is there is only so much that can be done through decorating and design and architecture—even if your budget is unlimited. If your vision is a wide-open living space, for instance, but you purchased a split-level home, there is a substantial gap between what you want and what is possible.

A new build is never going to feel like a 300-year-old apartment in Lisbon. Creating soulful interiors in recently built homes is something I do all the time. It can be achieved . . . up to a point. You can use reclaimed floors, add architectural salvaged items, choose historic hardware. The questions you have to ask yourself are: What concessions am I willing to make? Because you will have to make some. And is close, *close enough*—or should you look for a home that already has what you know you want?

---

1. **ANTIQUE COLUMNS.** Lauren bought a pair of old columns in the South of France. The finish is rustic, there's no shine, and there are pieces missing. The imperfections bring the character.
2. **OLD MANTELS.** We brought in an antique Louis XVI stone fireplace for a project in Cambridge, Massachusetts, that needed a strong historical element to contrast all the new drywall.
3. **ANTIQUE HARDWARE.** There is a feeling you get from old hardware that is almost impossible to replicate. This lion head door knob, original to the nineteenth-century home, represents a time when a front door always received special treatment.
4. **SALVAGED IRONWORK.** There are a pair of French Art Deco garden gates from the 1930s separating the kitchen from the dining room in this Palm Springs, California, home—the "something old" in a new construction.

1

2

3

4

ABOVE: The very beautiful—and unused—formal dining room in our Los Angeles home.

RIGHT: A different angle of the same space in its second iteration: a multifunctional family room/library.

REALITY CHECK

HOW DO YOU *REALLY* SPEND TIME IN YOUR HOME?

Take a moment to be very honest about how you live in your space. No fear of judgment. No getting caught up in the *should haves*—a house *should have* a formal dining room, a proper foyer, etc.

Where and how do you spend most of your time? Let your answer dictate the way you prioritize the design and budget. If the kitchen is where you'll be for 80 percent of your day, then open it up to the family room, if that is an option, or put a set of comfortable chairs and a side table in there, so when your best friend comes over you don't have to leave the space you love. (I spend most of my free time hanging out in our laundry room because I love how organized it is.) If movie night is an event the entire family shows up for, a big, comfortable sofa and a large television should be at the top of your list. Give yourself permission to invest in the areas that make you happiest, and don't be afraid to reallocate less frequently used spaces to help in those efforts.

When my husband and I bought our home in LA, we created an imposing formal dining room. It had a nineteenth-century English oak table, Jacques Adnet leather chairs from the 1950s, a lot of plants, and even more natural light—and we never went in there, ever. I would walk by, think to myself, "What a beautiful room," then continue down the hall. After a year, we decided to turn it into a family room/library, which we ended up using all the time.

Having a home that is perfectly in sync with how you move through it is one of the most beautiful ways to live.

2

EMBRACE HISTORY

A room does not feel special
unless it has old things in it.

A room does not feel special unless it has old things in it. If you take only one lesson from this book, let it be that. What old things bring into a space—history, a sense of discovery, nicks and imperfections—just can't be achieved when everything is new.

Buying all your furniture from the same store does—somewhat—guarantee a complete vision. But it isn't *your* vision: It will always lack heart, which can only come from taking the time to assemble an authentic mix. That means exploring and choosing things from different design eras, genres, and styles. Sorting what you like and being confident in those choices. Maybe a painted chest of drawers you saw on Chairish caught your eye. Do the work to figure out its origins. If it came from Sweden in the 1930s, for instance, search for similar examples. What other design doors does that open? Be curious.

There is a tendency to force people into specific style buckets, to corner them into only exploring one particular look: French farmhouse, Scandinavian, maximalism, minimalism, and on goes the list. You *do not* have to define yourself that way. In order to create an interior that feels layered and assembled and individual, one that breaks the barrier of uncertainty, it should include many different styles, and a mix of old and new. The only connection that needs to exist between one object and the next is that you like it.

My hope is that you learn to recognize when you're delighted by something. You may not understand what you love about it, but you know that if you left it where you found it, you would think about it for years to come.

PREVIOUS PAGE: My design partner Lauren's bedroom is a good example of how to introduce and balance historic elements: The mirror, an eighteenth-century gilded and carved Louis XV style, is hung above a fireplace that was made new for the room.

OPPOSITE: When an arrangement of objects is on the verge of feeling too polished, I like to bring in something from nature, an organic form to contrast the structure: a sculptural piece of coral, a geode, a selenite log.

WHY THIS ROOM

WORKS

Lauren's sunroom is a collection of furniture, objects, and choices that shouldn't work but sit together beautifully. There is a vintage Adrien Auduox and Frida Minet rope floor lamp, next to a custom sofa upholstered in a foliage-print fabric, next to a 1960s faux bois stone side table shaped like a tree. A stone garden sphere sits on the floor. Stripes are hand-painted on the ceiling. Woven tassels hang from the window treatments. The thread of connection is whimsy and craft; it comes together in an elevated way that feels both outdoors and in, a balance of natural materials set in a polished, elegant framework.

HISTORIC
REFERENCES

My obsession with old things began with an interest in history and is also tied to my childhood. My mother's home always maintained a certain balance. If there was a new coffee table, then there were old glass objects and vintage books on top of it. If she bought a new lamp, it found a home on an antique end table. Pairing opposites in this way creates a tension that I love.

The history of antique furniture, as recognized by most historians, dates back to the sixteenth century. That is hundreds of years' worth of makers reinventing the chair, the table, the chest of drawers. My mind jumps to this detail when I see a room full of pieces from the same era of design. Why—when there is so much to choose from, and get excited by—be so limited? It would be like living in New York City and only eating pizza. Not a lot beats a NYC slice, but you are missing out on everything else the city has to offer.

I understand that the world of antiques can feel intimidating. The options and information is vast—and some of the egos orbiting the space are even bigger. But the truth is, there are only two things you should listen to as you enter into these waters: your eyes and your heart. What do you see that you like? Would it make you happy if it were in your home? It's that simple. Having a base knowledge of design history will always be an asset. There is not a single piece of furniture being made today that was not in some way inspired by the past, including all the things that I design.

What follows, I hope, will spark your curiosity and introduce you to new ways of exploration. These lists are a compilation of my most commonly referenced eras of inspiration. They are a starting point for you to jump in, see what speaks to you, and start doing your own research.

10 FURNITURE STYLES TO CONSIDER

1 NEOCLASSICAL

APPROXIMATE DATES: Late 1700s

EUROPE

WHY I LIKE IT: The pieces are glamorous without being overwhelmed by curves.

DETAILS TO LOOK FOR: Gilded forms, historic architectural motifs, and rectilinear and square shapes with graceful, intricate carvings and subtle ornamentation.

THE PIECES: Large consoles, small benches, classic chests of drawers, armoires, bookshelves, dining tables, elegant mirrors.

THE NAMES: Jean-François Oeben, Martin Carlin, Jean-Henri Riesener.

WHERE TO SEE THIS STYLE: Get the Gusto, an antiques store in West Palm Beach, Florida; the present-day interiors of designers Stephen Sills, Darryl Carter, or Susan Ferrier.

2 LOUIS XVI

APPROXIMATE DATES: 1750–1800

FRANCE

WHY I LIKE IT: The clean lines and intricate carvings, inspired by ancient Greece and Rome (scrolls, columns, laurel leaves).

DETAILS TO LOOK FOR: Bronze accents; marquetry; rectangular shapes; and beautifully warm, gilded finishes.

THE PIECES: Dining chairs, small settees, benches.

THE NAMES: Georges Jacob, Jean-Henri Riesener, Jean-Baptiste-Claude Sené. These were the masters, whose pieces are mostly found in museums. Don't be afraid of "Louis XVI style," pieces by Maison Jansen, for instance, which are more affordable but not from this time period.

WHERE TO SEE THIS STYLE: The furniture of Marie Antoinette; the rooms at Fontainebleau and Versailles; and the modernist de Menil house in Houston.

3 FRENCH PROVINCIAL

APPROXIMATE DATES: 18th century

PROVENCE, FRANCE

WHY I LIKE IT: The wood furniture—old pine, walnut, oak—is uncomplicated, often with wicker or rush accents. I grew up surrounded by pieces from this era. My mother was drawn to the colors, textures, and graceful shapes.

DETAILS TO LOOK FOR: Clean, tapered legs, which I prefer to the American Provincial's more bulbous shape. Beautiful, timeworn finishes.

THE PIECES: Farm tables, carved armoires, dining tables, sideboards, small side tables.

A QUICK NOTE ON PAINT: Don't restore the original finish, nicks and shade variations are part of the charm.

WHERE TO SEE THIS STYLE: Any city with a French colonial past. Search dealers like French Antique Shop, Keil's Antiques, and M.S. Rau in New Orleans; Foxglove Antiques Collective and William Word Fine Antiques in Atlanta; and Joyce Horn Antiques in Houston.

4 SWEDISH/GUSTAVIAN

APPROXIMATE DATES: Late 18th century

SWEDEN

WHY I LIKE IT: The architectural carvings (diamonds, reeding, channeling) go well with neoclassical motifs.

DETAILS TO LOOK FOR: Original painted finishes in shades of cream, black, and gray, which can look chalky or very matte depending on the piece's age.

THE PIECES: Round center tables; gilded, painted wooden mirrors; classic oval or rectangular dining tables; stone-topped chests of drawers.

THE NAMES: Gottlieb Iwersson and Georg Haupt.

WHERE TO SEE THIS STYLE: The decor at Gustav III's Pavilion in Sweden. Swedish vendors on 1stDibs: Lone Ranger Antiques or Lorfords. The book *Classic Swedish Interiors* by Lars Sjöberg.

5 PRIMITIVE

APPROXIMATE DATES: 18th–20th centuries

CENTRAL AMERICA (ESPECIALLY MEXICO), PARTS OF SOUTH AND NORTH AMERICA

WHY I LIKE IT: I'm drawn to things that are made by hand, with uneven lines and imperfect forms.

DETAILS TO LOOK FOR: Dark wood in original finishes, simple shapes, and a tremendous amount of patination.

THE PIECES: Large dining tables; storage cabinets; sculptural objects, such as animal motifs.

WHERE TO SEE THIS STYLE: Casamidy, a furniture maker in Mexico; Chic by Accident and Daniel Liebsohn's Antiques and Eccentricities in Mexico City; a deep search on eBay or Etsy.

6 ART DECO

APPROXIMATE DATES: 1910–1939

UNITED STATES, FRANCE, SWEDEN, GERMANY, AND ITALY

WHY I LIKE IT: I'm drawn to the elevated finishes (detailed inlays, shagreen, marble, ebony) and the way they are married with simple, graceful forms.

DETAILS TO LOOK FOR: Rare materials like parchment, bronze, exotic woods, and high polishes.

THE PIECES: Cabinets and pedestals; interior hardware; plumbing fixtures; handwoven rugs; generously proportioned upholstery, like club chairs; light fixtures.

THE NAMES: Jacques Adnet, Jacques Quinet, Gilbert Poillerat, Émile-Jacques Ruhlmann.

WHERE TO SEE THIS STYLE: The de Noailles home in Paris designed by Jean-Michel Frank; Émile-Jacques Ruhlman's Grand Salon at the 1925 Paris Exhibition; the rooms on the Normandie ocean liner; Casa de Serralves in Porto, Portugal.

7 MODERNISM

APPROXIMATE DATES: 20th century

BELGIUM, SWEDEN, FRANCE, DENMARK

WHY I LIKE IT: These pieces are utilitarian but slightly more elegant with beautiful finishes and original hardware.

DETAILS TO LOOK FOR: Clean shapes made from nonprecious woods, like pine or even molded plywood.

THE PIECES: Cabinets, chests, armoires, bar carts, smaller settees, benches.

THE NAMES: Axel Einer Hjorth, Josef Frank, Poul Kjærholm, Charlotte Perriand, Le Corbusier, Hans Wegner, Fritz Hansen.

WHERE TO SEE THIS STYLE: Villa Savoye, Le Corbusier's modern take on a French country house, as well as his apartment in Paris; the book *Living with Charlotte Perriand* by François Laffanour; the Designmuseum Danmark in Copenhagen; Svenskt Tenn, an interior design studio in Stockholm, home to the Josef Frank archive.

8 1930S–1940S EUROPEAN

VIENNA, GERMANY, FRANCE, ITALY, SPAIN

WHY I LIKE IT: This is one of my favorite periods for almost every element in a room because of the graceful forms.

DETAILS TO LOOK FOR: Perforated metal panels; original glass features with detailed edges; lighter wood finishes; and materials such as leather, vellum, lacquer, and Murano glass.

THE PIECES: Curved sofas; occasional chairs that play with proportion, extra-high backs or extra-deep seats; architectural side tables; desktop accessories; mirrors; stone fireplace mantels.

THE NAMES: Pier Luigi Colli, Pietro Chiesa, Gio Ponti, Osvaldo Borsani, Ercole Barovier, FontanaArte, Guglielmo Ulrich.

WHERE TO SEE THIS STYLE: Villa Necchi Campiglio in Milan—a historic home, now also a museum—designed by the architect Piero Portaluppi.

9 EUROPEAN MID-CENTURY MODERN

APPROXIMATE DATES: 1950s–1960s

ITALY, FRANCE, SWEDEN, SPAIN, DENMARK

WHY I LIKE IT: There are such strong examples of shape and form, and an interesting mix of materials: iron and leather, bronze and old mirror, and limed oak open-grain finishes in different shades.

THE PIECES: Sofas and club chairs with linear shapes; low coffee and accent tables that mix stone and gilded finishes; floor screens; sideboards; desks; occasional tables.

THE NAMES: Axel Einer Hjorth, Jacques Adnet, Jacques Quinet, Pier Luigi Colli, Jean Royère, René Prou, Tommi Parzinger (a German-born American whose work was more closely tied to what was happening in Europe than the States).

WHERE TO SEE THIS STYLE: Maison Gerard gallery, Karl Kemp Antiques, and Pascal Boyer Gallery in New York; Exante Antiques in France; Marché Paul Bert at the Paris flea market.

10 1970S EUROPEAN

ITALY, FRANCE

WHY I LIKE IT: The humor! This furniture is whimsical and energetic.

DETAILS TO LOOK FOR: Experimental forms paired with an exploration of (then) new materials: fiberglass, molded metal, stainless steel.

THE PIECES: Low-slung seating; chrome on steel coffee and side tables; stone consoles and pedestals.

THE NAMES: Angelo Mangiarotti, Afra and Tobia Scarpa, Maria Pergay, Jacques Charpentier, Gabriella Crespi, B&B Italia.

WHERE TO SEE THIS STYLE: Design houses like Ligne Roset and B&B Italia; the Palm Springs Modernism Show; Demisch Danant gallery in NYC.

THE EXTRA CREDIT LIST

A few more furniture periods to look up and dive into:

- Baroque: Europe, 17th to mid-18th century
- Campaign Furniture: Britain, 18th and 19th centuries
- Empire: France, 1804–1815
- Vienna Secession: Austria, early 20th century
- Jugendstil: Germany, early 20th century

WHY THIS ROOM

WORKS

Our Los Angeles bedroom always felt like sleeping in a treehouse. There was a lot of history in that space. We brought back the sixteenth-century painting of St. Peter above the bed from Peru, where Jeremiah and I were engaged, and the frame is just as important as the portrait. The vintage tufted armchairs were in my first Chicago apartment over twenty-five years ago. The bedside tables are Italian from the 1970s. The light fixture, three pottery pendants by Georges Pelletier that we grouped together, are French also from the 1970s. The bed is new, and the rug is new—and the tension between the vintage and the new, along with a tight color palette, makes this room feel thoughtful.

5 LIGHTING STYLES TO CONSIDER

1 MID-CENTURY FRENCH

APPROXIMATE DATES: 1930–1960

WHY I LIKE IT: These fixtures always feel strong and confident in a space.

THE NAMES: Mathieu Matégot, Jacques Biny, Jean Royère, Jacques Adnet, Serge Mouille, Charlotte Perriand.

HOW TO LIVE WITH IT: Give them their moment. You don't need ten examples; one or two is enough.

2 MID-CENTURY ITALIAN

APPROXIMATE DATES: 1935–1965

WHY I LIKE IT: There is a strong utilitarian feel, with powder-coated metals and aged brass fittings. I respond to the architectural shapes, a lot of which have articulating—movable—arms, and frosted or green glass details.

THE NAMES: Pietro Chiesa, Castiglioni, Stilnovo, FontanaArte, Gio Ponti.

HOW TO LIVE WITH IT: This period plays well with classic antiques and historical architecture.

3 1970S LIGHTING

UNITED STATES, ITALY, SWEDEN, NORWAY, FRANCE, SPAIN, JAPAN

WHY I LIKE IT: Everything from this era feels irreverent and joyful. I'm drawn to the interesting use of materials: Plastics, Lucite, colored glass, Murano glass, washi paper.

THE NAMES: Verner Panton, Isamu Noguchi, Maria Pergay, Pierre Cardin, Gaetano Sciolari, Poul Henningsen, RAAK, vintage IKEA.

HOW TO LIVE WITH IT: The bold colors and expressive shapes mix well in a room with luxe materials like limed oak, walnut, leather, and brass. Look at any of designer David Hicks's interiors for reference.

4 STONE OR MARBLE LIGHTING

APPROXIMATE DATES: 20th century

UNITED STATES, ITALY, SPAIN, PORTUGAL, MEXICO, UNITED KINGDOM (ESPECIALLY ENGLAND)

WHY I LIKE THEM: The way light filters through stone, especially alabaster, creates a warmth that can light up a room with a single example.

HOW TO FIND THEM: There are not designer names attached to this category, instead search by material (alabaster or marble), place of origin (see above), or fixture type (table lamp, ceiling light, wall sconces, etc.).

HOW TO LIVE WITH THEM: Even in the most modern space, a classic stone lamp is in harmony with the interior. Try a pair of columnal lamps over a nineteenth-century painted chest of drawers.

5 OUTDOOR LANTERNS (FOR INDOORS)

APPROXIMATE DATES: 1800–1940s

UNITED STATES; EUROPE; CENTRAL OR SOUTH AMERICA, ESPECIALLY MEXICO; OR NORTHERN AFRICA

QUICK HISTORY LESSON: In the first part of the twentieth century, most outdoor lighting was made by hand from metals (bronze, iron, copper) that age beautifully.

WHY I LIKE THEM: When you bring something that's lived outdoors for years into your home, it contrasts the newness of the materials around it. Don't touch the finish. If the glass is damaged or the chain isn't long enough, try to replace them with versions that match the original parts.

HOW TO FIND THEM: Search by place of origin (see above) or material (also see above) on Etsy or eBay, or try your local architectural salvage yard.

HOW TO LIVE WITH THEM: If there is fresh paint on your walls, hanging a "crusty" lantern is an easy way to add character to your space. A pair of them hung over a kitchen island, in a bedroom, in a foyer, over a dining table; all look great.

WHY THIS ROOM

WORKS

The budget for this dining room renovation was tight. We sourced most of the furniture and lighting from popular design stores and Etsy. This space works because the vintage and antique objects bring in history. The pottery with imperfect finishes, the gilded mirror that's a little bit chipped. These were not expensive pieces, but they elevate the room and add so much character.

9 OBJECTS WITH CHARACTER TO CONSIDER

1 ART DECO RUGS

FRANCE, ITALY, SWEDEN

WHY I LIKE THEM: I have never been a fan of heavily patterned rugs. But there is something about the geometry and the limited palette of Art Deco rugs that I connect with, whether vintage or modern.

HOW TO LIVE WITH THEM: Woven from wool or silk, these rugs work well with mid-century European furniture, classic antiques, and finishes from the same era. I tend to reach for one in rooms that lean more minimalistic.

WHERE TO FIND THEM: 1stDibs; Doris Leslie Blau, a rug dealer in NYC; LiveAuctioneers.

2 ANTIQUE GILDED MIRRORS

WHY I LIKE THEM: This is a great entry point to antiques for anyone newly interested in old things. The character they bring to a space can't be replicated.

HOW TO LIVE WITH THEM: They work anywhere. When we lived in LA, a small gilded mirror hung above our entry table, which showed our love of mixing different eras.

WHERE TO FIND THEM: Start at your local antiques mall or flea market, where you're likely to find a deal. Scour eBay and Etsy.

3 VINTAGE SILVER FRAMES, CANDLESTICKS, & BOXES

SILVER FINENESS: Look for silver hallmarks, which indicate the purity of silver, typically stamped on the bottom of large pieces, like bowls, trays, or candlesticks. If the markings say .925 (Sterling) or .800 (Continental), you can be almost certain you are buying real silver.

WHY I LIKE THEM: Silver accessories elevate the things around them. They feel like heirlooms, even when they're not.

HOW TO LIVE WITH THEM: A beautiful coffee table book is great, but better when paired with a small silver box. Fresh flowers in a julep cup next to the bed. Framed family photos on the kitchen counter.

WHERE TO FIND THEM: Look for special pieces at flea markets, antiques malls, or in online auctions.

4 GLAZED OR HAND-PAINTED POTTERY

WHY I LIKE IT: You can play with the tonality of different glazes, allowing the texture of the finishes to stand out in a neutral space.

HOW TO LIVE WITH IT: I lean heavily into organic shapes that look old and feel handmade. A large, impactful grouping on a mantel (see page 25); or a bowl paired with other objects on a bookshelf; taller vases holding branches on a kitchen counter or entryway table.

WHERE TO FIND THEM: You can pick up pieces for $10 at your local antiques mall. Always be on the look out at vintage shops and flea markets, and on eBay and Etsy.

5 NATIVE AMERICAN BASKETS & TEXTILES

WHY I LIKE THEM: My fascination with things woven by hand, sewn by hand, dyed by hand started when I was a kid. Every home I've lived in has included nods to the crafting traditions of Indigenous American culture; it is a part of history that I am always curious to know more about.

HOW TO LIVE WITH THEM: Introduce objects in places where you least expect them: an Aztec pillow sitting on a modern club chair, or a grouping of beautiful baskets on top of an old armoire or on a shelf in your bookcase.

WHERE TO FIND THEM: Take the time to look for the genuine thing: New pieces that come from the craftspeople who made them, old pieces that still support the community. Stores like Shiprock in Santa Fe, New Mexico, and Mountain Lion Trading Post in Redondo Beach, California. The Santa Fe Indian Market, which happens each year at the end of the summer, includes over a thousand artisans.

6 MEXICAN POTTERY

WHY I LIKE IT: I have a deep, personal love for the pottery made in Mexico: the ceramic pineapples, with their distinct green and black and brown glazes; the rustic water jars, whose wear is proof of the purposes they served.

HOW TO LIVE WITH IT: They anchor a room. The unique forms and the handmade finishes contrast well with antiques that are more polished.

HOW TO FIND THEM: Mercado de Artesanías La Ciudadela, a local market filled with craftspeople and dealers in Mexico City; online at 1stDibs, Etsy, and eBay.

7 GEODES & MINERALS

WHY I LIKE THEM: There are people who believe in the healing powers of crystals and geodes, I just happen to think they are beautiful objects. Jeremiah and I used selenite logs and collections of geodes with white candles at our wedding instead of elaborate flower arrangements, because we decided we would rather spend money on something we could keep forever.

HOW TO LIVE WITH THEM: When I need "just one more thing" to make a shelf or arrangement feel complete, I reach for something from this category.

WHERE TO FIND THEM: You can spend a lot of money shopping for these, but you don't have to. I've found beautiful specimens at Home Goods for less than $12.

8 PRINTED LAMPSHADES

WHY I LIKE THEM: They are an easy upgrade that feels thoughtful. A fabric shade in a pretty pattern—or one that's hand-painted—is an opportunity to do something custom.

HOW TO LIVE WITH THEM: You have two options: pick a fabric that coordinates perfectly with everything else in the room, or find something unexpected and let it bring a pattern or color into the mix.

WHERE TO FIND THEM: Etsy, Chairish, or eBay. Fermoie, a fabric company in London. If you search "shade shop near me," there's likely someone who can make a lampshade for you (perhaps out of that patterned dress you no longer wear but still love).

THE EXTRA CREDIT LIST

A few more categories to look up that might spark your imagination:

- Peruvian textiles, new or old
- Eighteenth-century Grand Tour accessories
- Vintage Flemish tapestries
- Etchings
- Greek sculptures

9 CONTEMPORARY PAINTINGS

WHY I LIKE THEM: Paintings don't need to be from a renowned gallery. Pieces by a friend, a local artist, or a person whose work you discovered while traveling can be even more meaningful.

HOW TO LIVE WITH IT: Be free to live with what you love. Paintings don't have to coordinate with your room. When figuring out where to hang a particular work, consider what it brings to the moment—a statement at the end of the hall, an unexpected impact behind a seating area.

WHERE TO FIND THEM: Chance encounters and happy accidents—this is not something you leave the house looking for, as much as it is something you stumble upon and feel so lucky that you did.

Carlo Bugatti's "gong" chair (right) dates to the 1910s, and is one of those items that serious furniture collectors gravitate to and pay a lot for. I bought this one at auction, where I paid around 60 percent less than what a noted dealer or antiques shop would charge, and gave it to Jeremiah for his birthday. Also featured in this grouping: a vintage wrought iron floor lamp, a François Monnet bent steel table from the 1970s, a vintage Alabaster pyramid table lamp, and *Mirror*, a work by artist Richard Faralla, hangs on the wall.

SOME SOUND SHOPPING ADVICE

My first antiques were pieces I loved and could afford. A small vintage lamp, not a marble-topped console from the eighteenth century. Start small and stay open to new ideas. Antiques shopping is not a trip to the grocery store. You can't expect to head out with a list and find everything you want in a day. Things will find you more than the other way around.

The best deals are when the description is wrong. The tag says, "glass mirror," instead of "Venetian mirror," for instance, and is priced at $200, instead of $2,000. This is why a base knowledge of antiques is such an asset. Even if that mirror is not your style, you are now able to recognize it for what it's worth.

Here are some recommendations to help you on your hunt:

- Use the filter tool on larger sites (Chairish, 1stDibs, LiveAuctioneers) to see what is available locally, which cuts down on shipping costs.
- Google "local antiques malls." Visit them all.
- Get to know the high-end antiques shops in your area. Don't be afraid to reach out if you're looking for something specific. Everyone knows everyone in the world of selling antique furniture, so if they don't have an item, they will likely point you in the right direction.
- Don't be intimidated by the auction sites: Freeman's | Hindman, Doyle, Phillips, Christie's, and Sotheby's. When you are ready to make bigger investments, you can find special pieces and there are often deals to be had.

3

INTRODUCE CHARACTER

If it's been around since 1920 or earlier,
chances are it's a good option for your interior.

If it's been around since 1920 or earlier, chances are it's a good option for your interior.

Ask anyone at my firm what they hear me say most often (some might say too often) and it would be the sentence above. I've always been vehemently anti-trend. Here's why I think you should be, too: How many times have you walked into a room and felt like you are in another decade? You see cherry cabinets and green granite countertops. It's 1995. Oak cabinetry with a yellow stain. You're in the 1980s. Bright brass hardware. Hello, 1972.

My goal with any interior is to make it *un*-dateable. I look at rooms I designed twenty years ago, some of which are in this book, and they still hold up today (see pages 260 and 333). When it comes to construction materials and architectural features, I will always make the classic choice, pick the finishes with character that will stand the test of time. Spanish terracotta tile floors date back hundreds of years. You see them all over old European homes. Each time I use them in a new project they feel just as beautiful and timeless.

Despite the overwhelming list of design decisions that go into a project, there are places where you need to really stop and think about what building materials are going to make your house stay handsome forever. I always pause at hardware, fireplaces, floors, doors, and moulding—all of the foundational elements that add character and depth. These details set the tone for every other choice you will make, so ask yourself: Is there a vintage version? Is there an old option? The answer is likely yes; and, in my experience, it often costs significantly less—and was made better—than the bright and shiny and new.

PREVIOUS PAGE: The entry of our former NYC townhouse was fewer than 30 square feet. It came together detail by detail over time. The old brass hardware is from an architectural salvage yard. A set of antique, painted French metal doors, to which we added wavy glass panels, mark the transition into the main living area. The walls and ceiling have hand-cut antique mirror tiles. We captured the spirit of a grand, European estate in a space the size of a small closet.

OPPOSITE: It doesn't take a big architectural gesture to create character in your home. The smallest things can make an impact: A gilded medallion on a banister, a shaped edge on a stone countertop or backsplash. These details tell me that someone paid attention to every inch of their home and how it came together.

CREATING CHARM

I wrote about what it means to introduce character into a new home in chapter one, adding old mantels or architectural salvage in order to bring it to life. What you're *actually doing* by adding these details—by pausing and making thoughtful design choices—is creating an undateable interior. This foundation becomes a language for your home, even as the furniture and objects naturally evolve over time.

Few things are more rewarding to me than taking brand-new construction and layering in historic elements, installing an old limestone fireplace or adding crisp new baseboards over a worn stone floor. It allows you to mix the old with the new in a way that highlights the best of both.

If you live in an older home, you already have some charm and architectural history to work with. The aim, then, is to protect and preserve those elements. Restore rather than renovate. If you need to open up rooms because your galley kitchen is a traffic jam at mealtimes, that's what you should do. But use the existing historic elements as a guide. Save the profiles of the mouldings around the windows and doors and have them re-made to match. Find radiator covers that look like the originals. Be sensitive to the history.

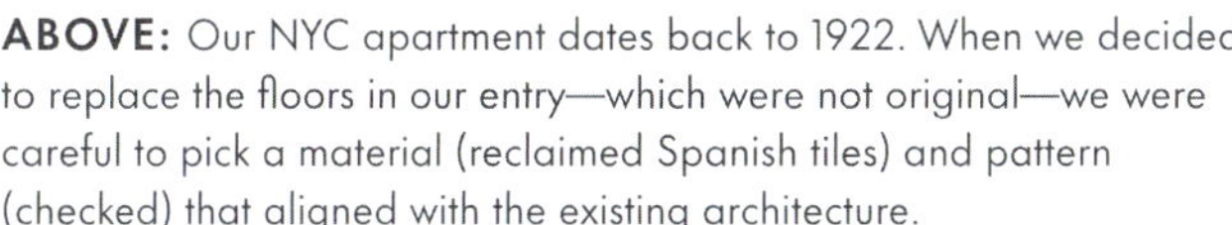

ABOVE: Our NYC apartment dates back to 1922. When we decided to replace the floors in our entry—which were not original—we were careful to pick a material (reclaimed Spanish tiles) and pattern (checked) that aligned with the existing architecture.

RIGHT: In contrast, this project in Palm Springs, California, was a custom build. When everything is new, some elements should be old. Antique mirror tiles and a pair of Art Deco iron garden gates fitted into the wall add character.

THE DETAILS THAT MATTER: HARDWARE

1

2

3

When my husband and I were renovating our home in Los Angeles, I spent days at Liz's Antique Hardware, digging through old door knobs and pulls. If you're not familiar with the La Brea institution, it is owned by Liz Gordon, a true aficionado in the world of antique hardware, and filled with over a million hinges, handles, knobs, pulls, and latches. I was on a mission to find enough sets of door knobs for all our interior doors, and pulls for our refrigerator and freezer. My fingernails were black and I loved it.

Hardware is a tactile experience as much as it is a visual one. Each time you open a drawer, close a cabinet, lock the door, you are interacting with a piece of hardware. To treat this decision as purely functional is to miss an opportunity to create a lasting connection in your space. Having special pulls that you've carefully considered can elevate the way you live. You can read my story about buying hardware in Greece on page 28.

1. The salvaged refrigerator door pulls, an English style from the 1920s, I found at Liz's Antique Hardware.

2. Our doors have an aged brass rim lock, a design from the late nineteenth century.

3. This pull is new, but the design dates back to the Art Deco period. I use contemporary hardware made to look old all the time, as long as the finish looks convincingly aged.

SOME SOUND SHOPPING ADVICE

Hardware is a good entry point for anyone interested in architectural salvage. It is easy to search for on Etsy or eBay and typically not a very big investment. Try local dealers first (architectural salvage yards, antiques malls, flea markets), and keep these tips in mind on your search:

- Choose pieces that match. Slight shifts in shape should be expected, but this isn't *that* dinner where everybody's got a different plate.
- Make sure backplates lie flush with a flat surface.
- Reach out to the people who work at antiques and architectural salvage shops if you're looking for something specific. Most are experts at locating the needle in the haystack.
- Ask if new screws can be aged to match the finish of your old hardware. If the seller won't do it for you, search online for aging solutions specific to your type of metal.

When you reach the stage of a project where you are choosing interior doors, you will likely weigh decisions about profiles, materials, and styles. Also consider vintage doors. Not every door in the house needs to be reclaimed. (Though, if you have the bandwidth and the budget to pull it off, it will be spectacular.) I position old doors in key places: to direct the eye to a special entrance, or highlight an area in a home, like the pantry, primary bedroom, or office.

Our NYC townhouse had a secondary set of painted, nineteenth-century French metal doors in the foyer (see page 70). They were purely decorative, a welcoming gesture inviting you into the rest of the home. We used a salvaged pine door instead of a garden gate in our former Los Angeles home.

Using reclaimed doors often takes a few additional steps. They may need to be shaved down to fit, the frame has to be newly made, and the hinges often need replacing. But I have always found the payoff to be well worth the effort, and I think you will, too.

A set of nineteenth-century, salvaged French doors draw attention to the entrance of this primary suite.

SOME SOUND SHOPPING ADVICE

I wish I could walk the hills of southern France in search of vintage doors that match. But the easier way to shop for old doors requires a visit to your local architectural salvage yard or some serious research online. Pricing, unfortunately, is all over the place. Doors can be $200 or $20,000. So spend time comparison shopping, and make sure you're walking away with the best deal. Please also consider the following:

- Doors that are slightly larger than the dimensions of your frame can be trimmed down to fit. Make sure you won't be cutting off important details. Avoid a situation where you have to build up a door that is too small.
- When using a reclaimed door outside, add a clear coat of matte marine finish to protect it.
- If you have old doors, stripping them and leaving them raw is beautiful.
- Try broad search terms like "salvaged interior doors" or "vintage doors" to start. Then filter by place of origin once you've determined the style that suits you: France, Mexico, Morocco, etc.

Fireplaces are an obsession of mine. The power of this single, salvaged moment to change the way a room feels cannot be overstated. A space could have new walls and new floors, but add this one old element—a salvaged fireplace surround—and the room instantly has a focal point with character.

I have never wavered on the importance of this architectural detail. When I bought my first Chicago apartment many years ago, I couldn't afford to make a lot of structural changes. A French, eighteenth-century limestone mantel was the one thing I chose to invest in, even over installing central air-conditioning. A choice I never regretted, even at the height of summer.

(Turn to page 134 to learn more about fireplaces and their components.)

For our home in Los Angeles, we brought in a Louis XVI limestone fireplace, found locally at Lebert Antiquities, and lined it with reclaimed Belgian firebricks laid in a classic, period-appropriate, herringbone pattern.

SOME SOUND SHOPPING ADVICE

There are dealers all over the world who find and remove old fireplaces to sell, so there is always a steady stream of new inventory to be explored. Pricing, however, can be a bit arbitrary. Shop around, compare quotes, and most importantly, look as close to home as possible. This is a heavy item, so if it can arrive by truck—as opposed to boat—you can avoid high shipping costs. Here are some other tips:

- Most of the furniture periods in the previous chapter have a specific fireplace style. Start by searching the eras you are drawn to.
- Country of origin is also a good jumping-off point.
- Measure your firebox. Check it twice. Only look at mantels that are *bigger* on all sides. There are ways to fill the space between an existing firebox and a larger mantel to make it work.
- When buying a mantel online, ask to see pictures of the sides and back, and get details about installation requirements. How does the mantel meet the wall?
- An uneven back is not a deal-breaker. It does mean you either have to rout out the drywall where needed, or find a contractor to do an even cut.

1

2

The first thing you need to know about installing reclaimed flooring is that it can be tricky, and that it is never going to be a bargain. Here's why I think you shouldn't let that scare you off: an old floor in new construction gives some much-needed authenticity. There's friction when you contrast timeworn flooring in a new room. Even if only used in a small area—a powder room or foyer, for instance—it is a worthwhile investment in the character of your home.

1. Architectural historians have traced the use of black-and-white checked tile to the grand public buildings and private estates of the Roman era (8th century BC). Inspired by the classic pattern, we re-created a version for a client using new Jura limestone and Nero Marquina marble tiles.

2. There are several companies who are very good at making newly cut tiles look old: Artistic Tile, Paris Ceramics, Exquisite Surfaces. Stones that are honed—sanded to create a flat, matte finish—and tumbled (shaken in a container of water and sand to achieve a weathered surface) are the most convincing. The herringbone tiles you see in this hallway are a great example.

SOME SOUND SHOPPING ADVICE

If your dream is to live with reclaimed flooring, then you will need to work with an expert who specializes in this material, and hire a talented installer (ask a showroom for their recommendations). This is not the time to bargain hunt or try to do it yourself. There are too many variables involved. The tradespeople in this field are the best at what they do, which is exactly what you want when committing to a design detail in this price range.

The easier and more cost-effective option is to use *new* flooring that's made to *look* old. We do this all the time in our projects. Consider one of the following materials, which have all had a place in design history since the 1920s:

- Oak floors, distressed or not
- Bleached pine floors
- Hand-formed and -fired terracotta or ceramic tiles
- Stone flooring with hand-distressed edges
- Penny round ceramic tiles
- Engineered alternatives of the above

Order samples of the flooring you are considering. With engineered options, be sure to get a few samples. You want to see how the individual tiles or boards come together, and how the aged effect is varied to look authentic.

THE DETAILS THAT MATTER: MOULDING & TRIM

Given its rich history as a decorative highlight, it is easy to forget moulding's original purpose was to hide the imperfections where two interior elements meet—essentially an architectural bandage. Over centuries, these details evolved into elaborate statements used to create highly inventive spaces, like many of the historic Beaux-Arts buildings in France.

Gone are the days when there were thousands of people trained in the exquisite art of plaster. You can still get almost any custom design carved out of wood, but it is expensive and not typically where I choose to allocate the budget.

When I am designing a moulding plan, I start with a historic reference, an image of the style and details I like. Then I give that inspiration to a contractor, who uses catalogs from mass producers/retailers, like Dykes Lumber, to piece together the look. You will likely need to combine a few different shapes to get what you want, but this is common. Just be aware that the more you can work with precut stock—as opposed to custom cuts—the more cost-effective your project will be.

---

1. The pediment over the door and the oval plaster on the ceiling are original and indicative of the Georgian architecture of this home.
2. Trim gives a flat wall texture and dimension. When you paint it a contrasting color the effect is more pronounced. I like to do this in small spaces, where it feels purposeful.
3. Picture mouldings make the ceiling feel taller and a space feel more sophisticated. They also take some of the guesswork out of where you should hang things.

SOME SOUND SHOPPING ADVICE

Work with an experienced contractor, but have your inspiration together before reaching out. I often start with more grandiose references and scale down for practicality. (Féau Boiseries, a French reclaimed paneling company, is a wonderful resource.) Here are a few other things to keep in mind when explaining your vision to a contractor:

- Ask to see a mock-up of the moulding and trim selections in your home. I *still* have a hard time imagining the outcome without seeing physical samples in a space.
- Check that the scale feels right: Is the combination heavy, light, or detailed enough? Are all the pieces proportionate to one another?
- Double-check impact: Does the combination say what you want it to?
- Live with it for a few days, if you can, before making final decisions. You want to get it right the first time.

THE DETAILS THAT MATTER: PAINT

If the goal is to create a historic connection in your home, paint is a good place to start. In the back of most paint decks you're likely to find a historical paint collection. (At Benjamin Moore, these are the shades that have numbers preceded by *HC*.) Those palettes contain colors and combinations inspired by a historical reference or place—Cape Cod, New England, Savannah, and so on. You can also check with your local historical society. Some towns keep a record of the colors that were originally approved for the exteriors of buildings, facades, and doors. Your paint store can match those shades for you.

Duxbury Gray, Benjamin Moore

Revere Pewter, Benjamin Moore

Lisbon, Portola Paints

OPPOSITE: Poppy and Oskar's NYC bathroom is painted a soft, grayish blue called "Lisbon" by Portola Paints, which was inspired by the color of the sea in that city.

MAKING CHOICES THAT STAND THE TEST OF TIME

In this chapter, I talked about materials and techniques from the past. Things that look and feel and are . . . old. I have spent a lot of years seeking out these timeworn elements, and the people who rescue them. The French race car driver in Los Angeles with a warehouse full of old building materials. The dealer at the Marché Paul Bert in Paris who specializes in antique lighting. These are some of my most-trusted relationships. I discovered them after years of relentless hunting, by following leads from hotel concierges and local shop owners, and by not being afraid to get lost in an unfamiliar city. I've listed here the phrases I use when searching for these architectural materials online, so you can start to find your own resources.

KEY SEARCH WORDS

1 CLASSIC HARDWARE FINISHES

Bronze

Unlacquered brass

Polished nickel

Blackened iron

Wrought iron

2 RECLAIMED DOORS

Antique painted doors

Vintage French doors

Rustic Mexican doors

Salvaged interior doors

Pair of antique doors

Vintage iron doors

3 OLD FLOORS

Reclaimed terracotta tiles

Vintage subway tiles

Reclaimed marble flooring

Old stone flooring

Reclaimed wood flooring: straight run, herringbone, chevron, distressed

4 SALVAGED FIREPLACES

Antique marble mantel

Antique stone mantel

Antique wood mantel

Reclaimed firebricks

Salvaged mantel

Salvaged Belgian roof tiles (in fireplace interiors)

5 MOULDING STYLES

Dentil

Louis XIV

Federal

Neoclassic

4

DEVELOP YOUR VISION

Train your eye to notice what it responds to.

Train your eye to notice what it responds to. As you begin your own renovation or decorating projects, finding inspirational images will help you develop and define your vision. These photos are an essential communication tool of any design process. If you are working with an interior designer, you will dissect these photos together, and talk about what you like, what you don't, and what you want to learn more about.

If you are taking on a design project yourself, this is even more important. For example, if you are thinking about custom built-ins for your family room, you *could* reach out to a cabinetmaker and ask them to build something with two sets of doors and four shelves, and they might come back to you with a plan that works. But is it going to be the design you wished for? Too much is left to interpretation. You will get where you hope to go faster—with fewer back-and-forths—by coming to a cabinetmaker with detailed photos and a vision for the wall. It is much clearer to point at a picture and say, "I like these doors, that moulding, this overall style, and that wood or painted finish."

Interior design is a visual experience, so it makes sense that we communicate best via a common visual language. Learning to speak it with some fluency will make the process of working with the people who can help you bring your ideas to life especially productive.

PREVIOUS PAGE: The concept for my design partner Lauren's powder room began with a single photo, an image of an old stone sink set inside an arch in an all-white bathroom. Her design then evolved into something richer and more layered, with terracotta walls, an aged gilded mirror, and Italian lights. The hand-painted border, something she saw on vacation, was the last detail added because she knew it needed "something more."

OPPOSITE: Lauren found a pair of eighteenth-century carved wooden cornices on LiveAuctioneers. Historically, a cornice sits horizontally above a doorway, window, or bed. There wasn't a place in her home that was wide enough to hang them in that way, so we improvised, mounting them together vertically on the wall.

THE EDITING PROCESS

Collecting imagery is *not* the only important part of gathering inspiration.

As fun as it can be to lose yourself in beautiful pictures, there is another key step in this process: editing. I have never had a client send me a picture of a room and ask me to re-create it exactly. Without exception, they all say, "I have photos, but I don't like everything in the image." Which is exactly as it should be. You're not supposed to.

Knowing how to dissect inspirational imagery is an essential part of educating the eye. Teaching yourself to register moments *within* a photo, as opposed to judging the room as a whole. The goal is to recognize, for example, that it is the sconces above the fireplace and the inventive seating arrangement, not the bright red fabric on the sofa, that keeps bringing you back to a particular living room.

When I look at images of rooms, sometimes it's just the layout, a way of positioning the furniture, that jumps out for me. Is there a round table in the corner with a chaise next to it? Or a folding screen, with a small painting hanging on it? You can skip over the color scheme, even ignore the style of the furniture. This is what a trained eye can take in, and where you will find valuable moments of inspiration.

SEEING THROUGH A DESIGNER'S LENS

On the next few pages, I will share some of my favorite inspirational photos, of both historical designs and new. I am going to explain what I see and don't notice when I look at each image, so that you can start to train your eye to do the same.

WHEN I LOOK AT THIS ROOM, I SEE . . . the clean lines of the furniture and the strict symmetry of the floorplan. I take in the singular pattern on the chairs in the space, and the multiple seating areas.

I DON'T FOCUS ON . . . the architectural materials: the thick rock columns, the heavy beamed ceilings, or the railings.

The Llao Llao Hotel in Argentina, designed by Alejandro Bustillo in the mid-1930s; Jean-Michel Frank 's furniture was used in the common spaces.

WHEN I LOOK AT THIS ROOM, I SEE . . . the marble door surround, and its relation to the pattern on the floor. I notice the floor, of course, and the three different colors of the door paneling.

I DON'T FOCUS ON . . . the green walls.

WHEN I LOOK AT THIS ROOM, I SEE . . . the classic shapes of the furniture and the mix of eras, and how together it feels modern. My eye goes to the painting and the negative space in the rug. I like how most of the floor covering is *not* patterned.

I DON'T FOCUS ON . . . the tone of the wood paneling or the bright colors.

Château de Groussay was built in 1815 in Montfort-l'Amaury, France, by the Duchesse de Charost. It was purchased in the 1930s by Carlos de Beistegui, an eccentric multimillionaire, who updated it with the help of architect and designer Emilio Terry.

Nelson and Happy Rockefeller's Fifth Avenue apartment, designed by Jean-Michel Frank in 1938.

WHEN I LOOK AT THIS ROOM, I SEE . . . the continuous pattern, how the same fabric is used on both the walls and windows. It feels modern to me, even though it is decidedly traditional. I also see an inventive use of an otherwise overlooked corner of a bedroom.

I DON'T FOCUS ON . . . the Turkish rug or the industrial style of the furniture.

Interior designer Muriel Brandolini's guesthouse in Long Island, New York, completed in the early 2020s.

WHEN I LOOK AT THIS ROOM, I SEE . . . the original architectural details and how the shape of the custom sofa references the wrought iron railings. The room has such great geometry and color.

I DON'T FOCUS ON . . . the pattern on the floor.

Interior designer Jacques Grange's Palm Beach, Florida, home, originally built in 1929, refreshed by Grange in the mid-2010s.

SEARCHING FOR
SIMILARITIES

Once you have a set of inspirational photos as a map for your design project, and you understand what it is that appeals to you within these images, take a step back and look with a wider lens. What similarities do you see? This expanded view may show you two things: Your style preferences could become more solidified, or you could find an entirely new style to explore. Are you attracted to neutrals and textures, for instance? Do handwoven accents resonate with you? Do you love pairs of chairs, pairs of lamps, pairs of tables? Do balance and symmetry catch your eye? Locking in your design perspectives, and highlighting what matters most to you will give you more confidence in your own taste and decisions.

First go narrow, then go wide.

SEEING THROUGH A WIDER LENS

If a client handed me this collection of photographs and asked me to create a room based on their selection, I would immediately know . . .

- They are not afraid of color, greens mixed with neutrals and grays.
- I need to embrace or create a lot of architectural character, use raised wood paneling, detailed moulding, and reclaimed materials.
- The room should feel assembled and collected, with a lot of different periods and styles mixed in. I would reach for hand-carved furniture, a lot of Louis XV–style pieces, but upholstered in a contemporary solid or subtly patterned fabric.
- They are open to whimsical details, like hand-painted ceramics and bolder textures.

INSPIRATION

IS EVERYWHERE, SO LET'S CAPTURE IT WELL

We have all walked into a restaurant, a store, a hotel, and thought: "I wish my home felt like this." These spaces are designed for that reason, to make you feel elevated, comfortable—at home. The next time you dream about how lovely it would be to live in the lobby of your favorite boutique hotel, pause and take in the details that matter to you. The tools you've learned can help you capture the mood and bring it into your own space.

Inspiration often comes from unlikely places. The patina on an old French bookcase. A sun-bleached shade of bricks on the sidewalk. The frame on a modern painting. If it catches your eye, try to catch it with your camera. Revisiting these moments when I'm feeling stuck creatively has a way of making me feel energized again. Here are some of my favorite sources of inspiration.

MUSEUMS AND HISTORIC SITES

WRIGHTSMAN GALLERIES AT THE METROPOLITAN MUSEUM OF ART IN NEW YORK CITY: One of the most important collections of French, eighteenth-century decorative arts and furniture.

THORNE MINIATURE ROOMS AT THE ART INSTITUTE OF CHICAGO: Compare historically accurate representations of different interior design styles in one gallery.

MUSÉE DE LA CHASSE ET DE LA NATURE IN PARIS: A stately private home that's been turned into a museum.

THE ACROPOLIS OF ATHENS: The majesty and proportions of the classic Greek architecture is almost overwhelming.

THE NEW YORK PUBLIC LIBRARY: A great example of architectural details that stand the test of time.

NEUE GALERIE NEW YORK: I have always loved the building, a Gilded Age example of grandeur, filled with incredible paintings and decorative art.

FURNITURE DESIGNERS

JACQUES ADNET: He used such beautiful materials: iron, alabaster, leather, parchment, and inlaid woods.

JEAN-MICHEL FRANK: Best known for the simple lines and quality of his furniture and lighting, and his confidence when assembling a room.

CHARLOTTE PERRIAND: Her work is a top representation of French industrial design.

PIERRE CHAPO: One of the most inventive furniture designers of his time, a master of shaping wood into beautiful forms.

MARIA PERGAY: She had a truly modern approach to shape, form, and humble materials, like steel.

INTERIOR DESIGNERS

JACQUES GRANGE: His ability to mix high-end things with whimsical elements and craft is something I admire.

MAISON JANSEN: A classic firm whose projects encompassed a lot of different styles, including the Kennedy White House.

JEAN-MICHEL FRANK (again and always): See above.

MURIEL BRANDOLINI: A friend and one of the most creative designers out there today.

ATELIER AM: There are few design firms whose projects I could personally move in to; this is one of them.

JEREMIAH BRENT: Watching his confidence and the evolution of his eye is endlessly fascinating to me.

HOTELS

THE CARLYLE: A New York City institution with interiors that feel not of this era.

HOTEL ESENCIA IN XPU-HA, MEXICO: A true example of laid-back luxury.

SÃO LOURENÇO DO BARROCAL IN MONSARAZ, PORTUGAL: The perfect example of why simplicity is always the best choice.

AMANTAKA IN LUANG PRABANG, LAOS: Our dream is to build a home inspired by its simple and elegant architecture.

RITZ PARIS: Arguably the most classic and timeless hotel in the world.

RETAIL EXPERIENCES

GALERIE HALF IN LOS ANGELES: The powerful curation and singular vision makes me want to have everything in my own home.

THE FUTURE PERFECT IN NEW YORK CITY AND LOS ANGELES: Leading the new wave of contemporary style.

RALPH LAUREN MEN'S FLAGSHIP IN NEW YORK CITY: Located in the Rhinelander Mansion, the space feels elevated but still comfortable at the same time.

IRENE NEUWIRTH JEWELRY IN NEW YORK CITY AND LOS ANGELES: These spaces demonstrate how design can be both whimsical and elegant.

PAVILION ANTIQUES IN CHICAGO: The owners taught me to love furniture through a new lens when I was in my twenties.

CASE STUDY

LIVING ROOM

We've talked so much about inspiration, finding it, capturing it, editing it. But what comes next? How do all of those "likes" become an actual room? This case study outlines the process my firm and I use to take a project from abstract inspiration to a fully realized interior, connecting the dots between moments found in images and things that show up in your home. I asked my design partner, Lauren Gordon, to walk us through these steps using her recently renovated living room as an example. Use this framework to put your own plans into action.

THE INITIAL INSPIRATION PHASE

Lauren's well-edited collection of inspirational photos, and why she chose them.

1. "Such an interesting mix of periods and styles: rustic antiques paired with modern art. It is a way to make old pieces feel relevant and fresh."
2. "My daughter, Georgia, sits in a French 1940s chair, something I already owned and loved."
3. "The rich brown of this upholstery and the way it contrasts so well with the neutral walls was something I was hoping to re-create."
4. "A young Jane Birkin with Serge Gainsbourg, both she and the stripes she's wearing are iconic."
5. "The columns with the French iron urns on them are the focal point of this arrangement. I like how they bring your eye into the corner of the room."
6. "The shape of this arch was a detail I shared with my architect, so we could replicate it throughout my home."

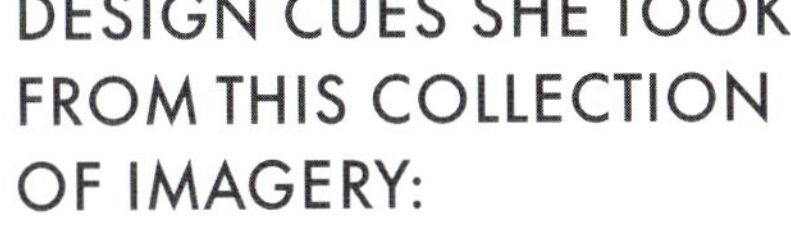

DESIGN CUES SHE TOOK FROM THIS COLLECTION OF IMAGERY:

- "Something needed to be striped."
- "I like light-colored walls."
- "There needs to be an interesting mix of antiques and vintage and new pieces."
- "Arched doorways are important to me."
- "I'd be more comfortable with a neutral palette, but I'm not afraid to mix in richer tones."
- "I want the French armchairs I already own to be present in this space."
- "I really love an old, chipping, gilded frame."

CASE STUDY

STYLE GUIDE

Based on her inspirational photo edit, here are some of the materials and key pieces Lauren was considering in her design.

WALL COLOR

Snowfall White, Benjamin Moore

TEXTILES

CLOCKWISE FROM THE LEFT: Striped fabric: Miguel in Stracciatella/ Liquorice, C&C Milano. Rich brown cotton/cashmere: Biarritz in Gilt, Rogers & Goffigon. Curly shearling, Edelman Leather. Floor covering: hand-loomed jute rug. Leather swatch: Oath by Ilse Crawford, Edelman Leather.

ARCHITECTURE

LEFT TO RIGHT: The fireplace: Lutyens Bolection, Jamb. The floors: Natural rift and quarter-sawn oak with a clear matte coat, no stain.

KEY FURNITURE PIECES

CLOCKWISE FROM THE LEFT: Custom sofa in this shape. Nineteenth-century French center hall table, Old Plank Antiques. Lounge chairs with English rolled arms. Vintage René Prou coffee table, 1stDibs.

KEY OBJECTS

LEFT TO RIGHT: Antique oil painting, J. Garrett Auctioneers. An antique French tapestry.

KEY LIGHTING

TOP TO BOTTOM: French, 1940s iron and gilt sconces by Raymond Subes. An antique lantern. A modern floor lamp.

CASE STUDY

FINAL DESIGN

Some of Lauren's original references evolved (she chose a different, darker stone for her fireplace surround, for instance), while others stayed true to the original inspiration (the striped fabric on her sofa). She sourced things from Etsy, her favorite galleries abroad, and antiques stores in Chicago. That's typical. As you put the pieces of a room together, some things you thought you loved fall out and new things are introduced. Stay open to these changes.

LEFT

MIRROR: French antique.

STOOL: French, 1950s ottoman.

TABLE: French, nineteenth-century center hall table.

RUG: Custom jute rug.

TABLE LAMP: Vintage Stilnovo lamp.

VASE: Vintage pottery.

OPPOSITE

CENTER CONSOLE: Vintage bronze bird table.

VESSEL ON TOP OF CONSOLE: Willy Guhl "Handkerchief" planter.

LOUNGE CHAIRS (LEFT): Vintage Jacques Adnet lounge chair in Biarritz Gilt fabric.

COFFEE TABLE BETWEEN LOUNGE CHAIRS: Vintage René Prou coffee table.

FIREPLACE: Lutyens Bolection in Nero Marquina marble.

SCONCES: French, 1940s iron and gilt sconces by Raymond Subes.

PAINTING ABOVE THE FIREPLACE: Oil on wood panel by Kyohei Inukai.

ARMCHAIRS: French, 1940s iron armchairs upholstered in curly shearling.

LANTERN: Vintage tole lantern.

PAINTING ON THE LEFT: Antique oil painting.

TAPESTRY: Antique French. **SOFA:** Custom in Miguel Stracciatella/Liquorice striped fabric. **COLUMNS:** Nineteenth-century English scagliola columns. **URNS:** Eighteenth-century French. **ARMCHAIRS:** Vintage Danish leather armchairs. **COFFEE TABLE:** Custom. **CUBE SIDE TABLE:** Custom. **FLOOR LAMP:** Vintage Italian. **ART ON THE RIGHT:** Acrylic on handmade paper by Alejo Palacios.

5

ROOMS FOR LIVING

6

ROOMS TO RESET

7

ROOMS TO GROW

8

ROOMS TO WORK

9

ROOMS FOR THINGS

PART 2

PUTTING IT INTO PRACTICE

Part one was about process. How to make design personal. How to include history and character in your home. Why the details matter. We walked through the steps of developing a well-thought-out vision for your space, one that reflects you and the way you live. Essentially, I tried to lay the foundation, and now it's *finally* time to start designing for yourself.

Part two is a room-by-room exploration of what it looks like when you put these ideas into practice. How, when you start to approach design in this way, your spaces feel more interesting, layered, and confident—and more like you.

This seating area has a tight, monochromatic palette, which gave Jeremiah and me the opportunity to assemble a collection of vintage furniture and objects and arrange them in a way that allows you to appreciate the interesting forms of each piece, instead of having your eye be distracted by a lot of color or pattern.

5 ROOMS FOR LIVING

Living Rooms | Family Rooms | Entries
Kitchens | Dining Spaces

LIVING ROOMS

The living rooms that stay with me, the ones that leave a lasting impression, feel both personal and unexpected. They are layered and assembled, with floorplans that are both livable and visually creative. A pair of armchairs, one at a casual angle, the other straight on, because you like to sit with your legs crossed and your partner does not, and the arrangement allows you to face each other while you rehash the day. When I consider some of the spaces that have inspired me—Jean-Michel Frank's sophisticated, historic interiors or the attention to detail found in rooms crafted by the legendary decorator Jacques Grange—there are certain elements that continue to jump out. Stylistically, the tone swings from traditional to modern, but these guideposts remain the same:

- A mix of seating that includes upholstery and architecturally interesting shapes.
- Texture, in what you touch and in the timeworn materials you see.
- Pieces that represent different eras, cultures, and movements in design.
- A floorplan that promotes conversation and highlights the architecture of the room.

RIGHT: If this living room looks familiar, you're not wrong. The design was inspired by the NYC townhouse Jeremiah and I renovated when we first moved back from LA. As with all inspiration, adjustments must be made to fit how you live in your home. For a family of four with two grown sons, the space needed to be more practical. The sofa is longer and the coffee table is larger, so that everyone would have a comfortable spot to land.

PREVIOUS PAGE: The breakfast room in my design partner Lauren's home is a quiet retreat away from high traffic areas. By bringing in elements of nature—ceramic light fixtures, a lot of stone and wood—it feels like you're sitting outside instead of in.

WHATEVER YOU DO, PLEASE DON'T . . .

- **BUY A MATCHING SET OF FURNITURE.** The convenience isn't worth the lack of visual impact.
- **COMMIT TO A PATTERN ON A LARGE PIECE OF FURNITURE** (unless you *really* love it). Save those moments for accent chairs or throw pillows, which are easier to replace if you get tired of the print.
- **SPEND TOP DOLLAR ON EVERYTHING IN THE ROOM.** There's an elegance that comes from curating a high-low mix.

The most important furniture purchase you make in a living room is the sofa. You need to consider comfort, function, and how and where it was made, but first you should understand how the shape will dictate the placement of almost every other piece of furniture in your space. Sofas determine the flow in a room, where people gather, and whether the mood leans more formal or intimate or casual. On the next few pages, we look at the choices—the pros, the cons, and some ideas for floorplans—to help make this decision more straightforward.

SOME SOUND SHOPPING ADVICE

A well-made sofa can last a lifetime. Eventually, it may need to be reupholstered or to have the cushions re-done, but the important parts—the frame, the springs—will stand the test of time. There are very few manufacturers still making sofas in the old way, but they are well worth seeking out and investing in: George Smith, Avery Boardman, Lawson-Fenning, and Jonas Workroom are a few my firm uses often. Here are some points to consider and construction details to look for before you buy:

- Sit on it. Not popular advice, given the current pull to find everything online. But trust me: mistakes are what keep Facebook Marketplace stocked.
- Check for straight seams on the frame and cushions, which is an obvious sign of quality.
- Read the small print. You want a fill that is not all foam and not all down, which will guarantee that your cushions keep their shape.
- Kiln-dried hardwood frames won't warp or bow.
- Don't let "the sit" of the cushions—whether they are too firm or too soft—be the deciding factor if you love everything else about a sofa. Cushions can be remade by a local upholsterer at your preferred firmness.
- Look for "hand-tied" or "eight-way hand-tied" construction, the technical description for how the springs connect to the frame. This structural web ensures everything stays where it is supposed to.

It can be hard to divide large rooms into zones. A curved sofa, which is pretty from all angles, will give you more options. In our Montauk, New York, living room, the curved sofa anchors a group of seating around the fireplace without blocking off the rest of the space.

YOU WANT A STRAIGHT-RUN SOFA IF . . .

a classic-but-curated floorplan is the goal. The shape gives you the freedom to do something less regimented, less symmetrical, less expected with the furniture around it.

ONE SOFA, TWO FLOORPLANS

TRIED-AND-TRUE

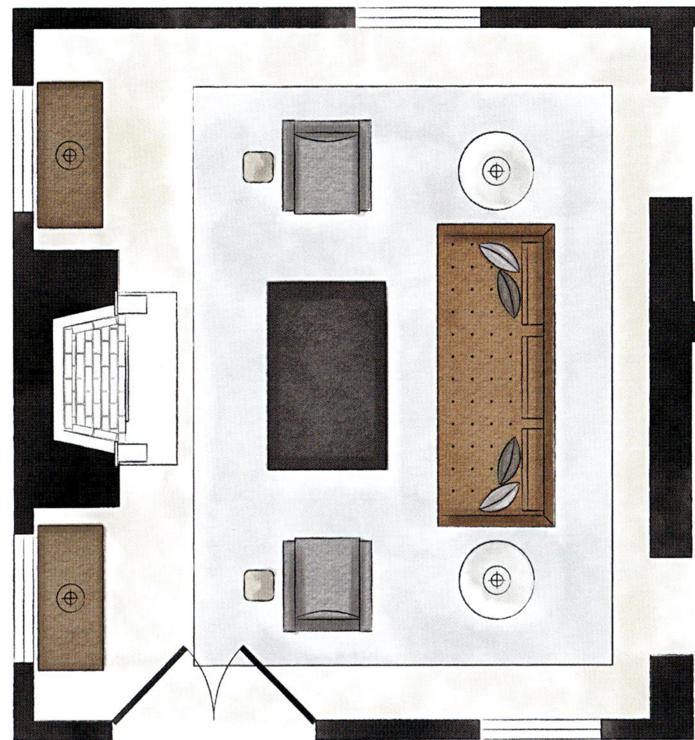

A combination that is in perfect symmetry; this room is easy to live in and promotes conversation.

LAYERED AND ASSEMBLED

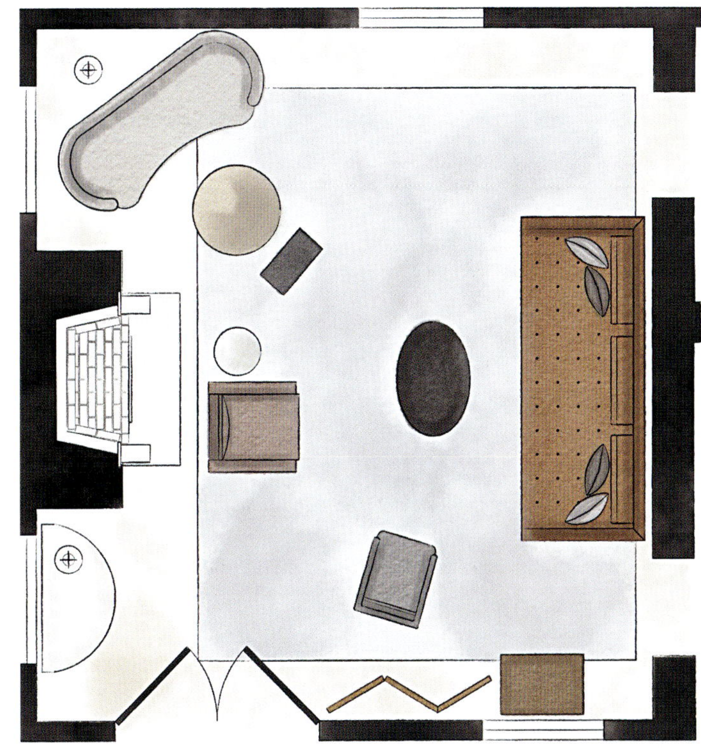

This grouping maintains balance without symmetry, and the smaller second sofa adds versatility.

YOU WANT A CURVED SOFA IF . . .

the aim is to visually break from the linear patterns of the architecture. It makes a room feel more intimate. The angle provides an opportunity to work in things like decorative screens and architectural floor lamps, and can allow multiple seating areas, as opposed to one large furniture arrangement.

ONE SOFA, TWO FLOORPLANS

TRIED-AND-TRUE

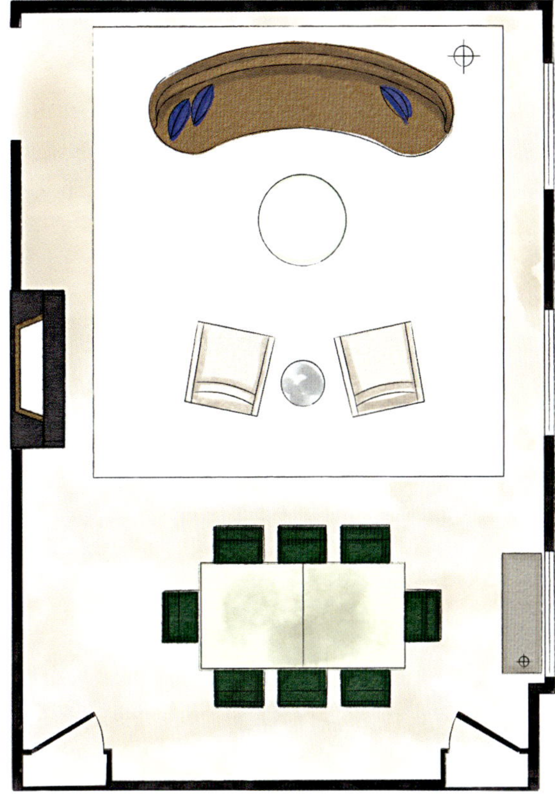

A pair of architectural armchairs facing a gently curving sofa allows maximum entertaining in this great room.

LAYERED AND ASSEMBLED

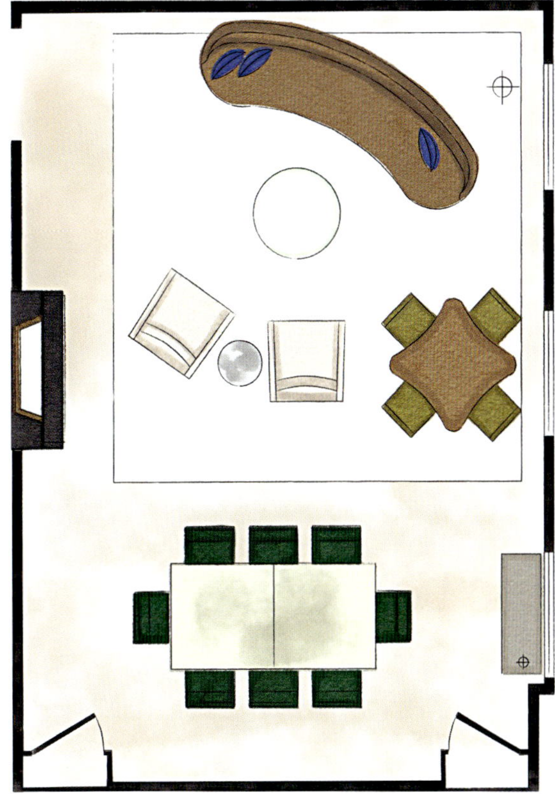

The curve of the sofa is what allows you to visually take in this multi-functional layout, helping your eye skim across the whole room.

YOU WANT AN L-SHAPED SOFA IF . . .

the mood is casual, you need to maximize seating, and you don't want to add a lot of additional furniture. (This is also true for modular or U-shaped sofas.) I suggest this style when designing for large families who gather in the living room to watch movies or play games. The vibe is laid-back and inviting.

ONE SOFA, TWO FLOORPLANS

TRIED-AND-TRUE

Simple and streamlined, this minimalistic approach—one large sofa, a coffee table, and a pair of side tables—feels casual while prioritizing seating and function.

LAYERED AND ASSEMBLED

This space could easily handle a curved sofa, but using an L-shaped configuration instead brings down the formality.

UP YOUR PILLOW GAME

Making a conservative fabric choice for large pieces of furniture is a smart move. The investment is too high to choose something you could get tired of in a year. That doesn't mean you have to avoid patterns, colors, or texture in the other elements of a room; introduce those details through decorative pillows, which are easier to swap in and out, and a safer way to be more adventurous.

1. **PAIR THEM UP AND SPREAD THEM OUT.** With long sofas, I group two pillows, usually 20- or 22-inch squares, and keep a similar distance between groupings.
2. **LAYER DIFFERENT PRINTS AND PATTERNS BUT PAY ATTENTION TO SCALE.** A tight geometric check and a loose floral work well together.
3. **TEXTURE CAN BE JUST AS IMPACTFUL AS PATTERN.** Try something with a heavy weave if your sofa or chair is upholstered in a flatter fabric, like cotton, linen, or velvet.

UPHOLSTERY UPGRADES THAT ARE WORTH YOUR TIME AND MONEY

If this were the nineteenth century, you wouldn't find a decorative pillow that didn't include some dressmaker details. I use them all the time on sofas, headboards, pillows, drapery, and lampshades. They feel finished and thoughtful in a modern room. Here are a few of the trims I reach for most often:

- Contrast leather welting
- Self-welting
- Tassels
- Fringe
- Decorative tape
- Embroidery
- Box pleating

I look for the strongest contrasts in a room, pairings that wouldn't traditionally go together but somehow make a space feel layered and interesting. Designers like Andrée Putman were doing this in the 1960s in Paris: creating modern furniture groupings in classic architectural shells. Our NYC living room was also inspired by this idea. The classic bones are original: ornate moulding, chevron floors, and highly detailed millwork. What we brought into the space is not classic at all. Instead of a painting or a mirror above the mantel, Jeremiah hung a vintage, linear light bar. The French slate table in the corner, which holds many meaningful objects, was originally meant to be outdoors. There is a constant push and pull between the modern, rustic, and ornate.

LET'S TALK ABOUT COFFEE TABLES

"Scale" is a word you hear a lot from interior designers, especially when discussing how a piece of furniture relates to another. It's always been a tune-out word for me, though. As a concept, scale is too abstract, too hard to define in a helpful way. Instead, when choosing a coffee table, I consider shape, material, and quantity—and let function be the deciding factor. This frees you to play with proportion and height, whether you go with something very narrow, or slightly lower or higher than the seat of your sofa.

1. **INTRODUCE A DIFFERENT STYLE.** The two heights and angular edges of this marble table catch the eye in a way that something more traditional wouldn't; a very modern element in a classically appointed interior.
2. **TRY SOMETHING PETITE AND ARCHITECTURAL.** The smaller size of this steel table goes against convention, which feels fresh.
3. **BRING MORE MATERIALS INTO THE MIX.** Glass and wrought iron lighten a room full of heavier upholstery.
4. **PLAY OFF OF THE SOFA SHAPE.** This small, circular table tucks into the curves of the sofa, keeping the open flow through the room.
5. **MARBLE IS ALWAYS A COMPELLING CHOICE.** Instead of anchoring this enormous room with a large sofa, we chose to group the seating around a generously-sized stone table.
6. **SOMETIMES THREE IS BETTER THAN ONE.** If you have a long sofa, there's something unexpected about doing individual, smaller tables grouped together. The room doesn't feel overwhelmed by large furniture.

JAPANESE INTERIORS
1

2

3

4

5

6

STYLING GUIDE

THE COFFEE TABLE

There are no rules for what to put on a coffee table. I love a curated mix of books and objects and things that tell your story. Think about the different eras of design you connected with in chapter two. How can you use those influences on your coffee table in a personal way?

ALMOST MAXIMALIST. The warmth of this marble table led me to books that have beautiful, patterned covers and to a mix of bronze and glass objects.

MIX YOUR MATERIALS. This rustic wood table has something brass, something stone, and something linen—both soft and hard finishes.

BOOKS MAKE GREAT SURFACES FOR CURATING OBJECTS; a grouping of smaller things feel more impactful.

IT'S OKAY TO KEEP IT SIMPLE, especially on a glass-top table where too many objects can feel busy.

A BEAUTIFUL TRAY IS PRACTICAL. You can quickly slide an arrangement off the table when you need more surface area.

PLEASE PAUSE FOR
NOMA

In this Chicago home, the original mantel was imposing enough that it allowed us to be looser with the furniture placement. None of the seating faces the mantel intentionally, so we could create multiple places to gather.

FIREPLACES

If you have a fireplace in your living room, it will be a focal point—but not necessarily the *only* center of attention. Your furniture doesn't always have to be facing it in an admiring semicircle. Consider creating a second, more intimate, seating area. Sometimes all this grouping needs is two comfortable chairs, whether they match or not, or a pair of well-crafted benches.

ANATOMY OF A FIREPLACE

The decorative parts of a fireplace typically include these four components:

- **FIREBOX:** The opening where the fire is built.
- **MANTEL:** The ornamental frame around your firebox.
- **SLIP:** The space between your mantel and the firebox, usually 16 to 18 inches, meant to protect your room from the fireplace's heat.
- **HEARTH:** The fire-resistant flooring directly in front of the fireplace.

The very first eighteenth-century French limestone mantel I bought from Mary Jeanne for my Chicago living room.

MARY JEANNE KNEEN

In this Chicago home, the original mantel was imposing enough that it allowed us to be looser with the furniture placement. None of the seating faces the mantel *intentionally*, so we could create multiple places to gather.

FIREPLACES

If you have a fireplace in your living room, it will be a focal point—but not necessarily the *only* center of attention. Your furniture doesn't always have to be facing it in an admiring semicircle. Consider creating a second, more intimate, seating area. Sometimes all this grouping needs is two comfortable chairs, whether they match or not, or a pair of well-crafted benches.

ANATOMY OF A FIREPLACE

The decorative parts of a fireplace typically include these four components:

- **FIREBOX:** The opening where the fire is built.
- **MANTEL:** The ornamental frame around your firebox.
- **SLIP:** The space between your mantel and the firebox, usually 16 to 18 inches, meant to protect your room from the fireplace's heat.
- **HEARTH:** The fire-resistant flooring directly in front of the fireplace.

The very first eighteenth-century French limestone mantel I bought from Mary Jeanne for my Chicago living room.

MARY JEANNE KNEEN

Mary Jeanne Kneen is singularly responsible for my deep love of reclaimed fireplaces. I went to her when I bought my first Chicago apartment, and was insistent that the limited renovation include an antique mantel. Her company, in the early 2000s, had an incredible selection of salvaged fireplaces. She graciously worked with me to find something within my very tight budget, and then went the extra step of explaining, piece by piece, what the slip would be made of, how the firebox interior should be tiled, showing me for the first time all of the pattern options and historical inspiration. I have not forgotten the lesson or passed on an opportunity to put it into practice.

Mary Jeanne now owns Kneen and Co., a beautiful showroom on Michigan Avenue that focuses on luxury tabletop goods and decorations—though she still carries a handful of beautiful stone mantels from Europe. She was kind enough to share with me some of what she's learned in her twenty-five years of salvaging and selling antique fireplaces. Here are her thoughts:

YOU DON'T HAVE TO MATCH THE STYLE OF YOUR FIREPLACE TO THE ARCHITECTURE OF YOUR HOME. Instead, I ask clients to tell me about their palette. Is it cool colors? Something warmer? Then I suggest mantels that work with those shades, whether it means finding something that blends in or something with the right contrast.

MY FAVORITE FIREPLACE STYLE IS LOUIS XIV FROM THE EARLY EIGHTEENTH CENTURY. I had one in the house Nate helped me design in Chicago. It was a beautiful shade of gray with just a little bit of blue and heavy ornamentation.

THE BIGGEST MISTAKE PEOPLE MAKE IS ONLY THINKING ABOUT THE MANTEL, which is just a pretty picture frame, really. What about the components inside: the firebox, the hearthstone, the slip, the firebricks that line the firebox? I like to use reclaimed materials for these details, firebricks and stone that historically you would have seen with the period your mantel dates to.

MAKE SURE YOU ADHERE TO YOUR LOCAL FIREPLACE CODES. Every county has different regulations, and it's really important to get this right. Find an experienced mason in your area to work with.

STYLING GUIDE
THE MANTEL

If you can only keep one surface in your living room looking pristine amidst the chaos of a busy life, make it your mantel. This is not the place for keys or yesterday's mail. It is an opportunity to bring out your best design ideas, to reach for objects and lighting that excite you, and to arrange it all in a way that is compelling and edited.

Consider a collection of objects.

Consider an asymmetrical arrangement of objects or hanging artwork off-center.

Consider a single sculptural moment.

ORIGIN STORIES

What's most interesting to me about this candleholder is the story behind its shape. It is counterweighted, so the candlestick moves up or down based on where the base sits. Originally designed during the Arts and Crafts movement, it was meant to sit on top of a piano and lean over the edge to illuminate the keys.

THE MOMENTS
THAT MAKE THE ROOM

DO YOUR OBJECTS TELL THE STORY OF THE PLACES YOU LOVE, whether you've traveled there or simply wish to? Embroidered textiles from South America. Baskets from Southeast Asia. Pottery from Peru. Wherever it is that interests you, find out what the local craftspeople are best known for and add it to your space. The handmade, imperfect finishes of these pieces add a layer of character that can't be replicated.

SELECT PAINTINGS, DRAWINGS, AND PHOTOGRAPHY WITH A PERSONAL CONNECTION, something that reminds you of a loved one, a place, a time that makes you smile. We have my late partner Fernando Bengoechea's woven photographs hanging in our home for this reason. Few things are better than walking through a room and being reminded of some of the memories that matter.

DECIDE WHERE YOU NEED SIDE TABLES. If something feels like it's floating in the room, it likely needs a surface next to it. Once you've made a furniture plan, imagine yourself in that space with another person. Where are you both sitting? Where are you putting down your coffee? If you have four friends over, where do the wineglasses land? No one should have to cross a room to set down a drink.

CHECK YOUR MATERIALS. Is there at least one representation of the following elements in your space: wood, metal, stone, glass, and something heavily woven? You need this diversity, the contrast of warm against cold, soft against hard. It's how you build texture into your design.

MY BEST ADVICE ON WHERE TO SPEND & WHERE TO SAVE

SPEND ON . . .

- The sofa
- A coffee table
- Case goods, like bookcases or cabinets
- Lighting
- Great vintage accessories

SAVE ON . . .

- Window treatments
- Rugs
- Decorative pillows
- Side tables
- Occasional chairs

FAMILY ROOMS

Always more casual than living rooms and a little more personal, too, family rooms are softer and warmer, the place to land for an afternoon nap. They are often designed around a television—let's be open about that. But don't allow watching a screen to be the *only* activity you plan for in this space. If you play cards or a lot of board games, is there room for a game table in front of a window with four chairs? If you are a family of readers, have you included enough comfortable seating with direct lighting? The most critical goal for these rooms is ease and versatility. Here is how my firm and I accomplish that:

- A floorplan that works for Sunday morning cartoons, along with everything else you do in this space. (Turn to page 146 for examples.)
- The surfaces are on the generous side: sofas are a touch deeper, coffee tables a touch wider.
- Sturdy side tables are essential.
- Include a mix of lighting for different times of day and night activities. (See page 156.)
- Bookshelves that hold more than books: vintage accessories, small objects, collections, or framed family photos.

Family rooms need to be versatile, and modular seating is an easy way to achieve that. The components of our B&B Italia sofa are constantly shifting depending on how we are using the room.

WHATEVER YOU DO, PLEASE DON'T . . .

- **SACRIFICE PERSONAL STYLE FOR UTILITY.** You may think a performance fabric feels too industrial, but there are some very luxurious options.
- **FILL THIS ROOM WITH THINGS THAT ARE TOO PRECIOUS.** Don't make yourself beholden to the finish of anything in a family room.
- **ONLY POSITION FURNITURE FACING THE TELEVISION.** A screen should not be the sole focal point of the space.

CASA SAN MIGUEL
mexico
The Popular Arts of Mexico
X RAY
LOVING
ANDY WARHOL
Polaroids 1958–1987
Creature

ABOVE: We included an old marble coffee table in our family room in Montauk, New York, because nothing our kids do can hurt it, including dance parties before bedtime.

OPPOSITE: The family room requires as much comfortable seating as possible and plenty of surfaces to set things down on. This cabinet is the exact size of the back of the sofa for that reason; it's an easy landing spot for a book or a bowl of popcorn.

CONSIDERING ZONES

Family rooms need to be hardworking and comfortable. A place for gathering, but also where several people can do multiple activities at the same time. Take this into consideration when mapping out your floorplan. What are you doing in this space? What furniture do you need, and how can it be arranged to maximize function? If homework or a quiet spot to read are a priority, is there a way to tuck a desk or chair into a corner away from the distraction of the television? Be intentional in your planning and try to take advantage of every corner.

DO YOU HAVE ROOM FOR . . .

1. **A GAME TABLE,** which doubles as overflow seating for dinner parties, or as a place to set out snacks or a bar when you entertain?
2. **AN INTIMATE CORNER SEATING AREA,** a place for guests to gather after the meal is over?
3. **A DESK AREA** for work-from-home days and schoolwork?

1

2

3

SO, WHERE DOES THE TV GO?

I have many clients who want their television front and center. But my advice is to try to be slightly more inventive, as long as no one is uncomfortable on movie nights. Would one of these places work in your space?

- To the left or right of the fireplace, instead of above the mantel.
- Tucked inside a piece of furniture with doors that close.
- Hanging on the wall surrounded by art or objects to create a collage.
- Built into custom bookshelves.

When mounting a television inside custom millwork, there are two considerations that will give your design longevity: including a place to hide electrical outlets and wiring that is easily accessible for repairs, and leaving extra hanging space around your existing television, so you can replace it in the future without having to find one that is the same size.

HIGH-FUNCTIONING FURNITURE

An ottoman as a coffee table works well in a family room. It doubles as seating, and there are no sharp edges to worry about if you have young children. This piece, a custom design by my firm in Chicago, includes a small built-in tray that pulls out so you can put down a drink or a bowl of popcorn.

ANOTHER THING . . .

Place screens as far away from natural light sources as possible to avoid glare, or invest in window treatments that can diffuse the afternoon light.

PLEASE PAUSE FOR

BOOK-SHELVES

A custom wall of built-in cabinetry is a design investment, like a kitchen renovation or stone countertops, that defines your home. In a family room, which is inherently chaotic, a wall of well-styled shelves might be the calmest moment in the space. When you look up and your eye lands on a beautiful arrangement of objects and books, it gives the space a sense of order.

The bookshelves in our NYC family room are beautiful and highly functional. The wall of shelves display our most cherished objects, while the row of gallery lights and the storage underneath allow us to control both the mood and the stuff.

Stephen Fanuka and I have worked together for over a decade. When I was hosting *The Nate Berkus Show*, we had a segment called "While You Were Sleeping," where the two of us would secretly renovate a room in someone's home overnight and surprise them in the morning. Thankfully, our recent renovations have a lead time longer than ten hours.

Stephen is a contractor and a second-generation master craftsman, and owns Fanuka, Inc., in Queens, New York. His work has a level of precision you just don't see from a lot of contractors these days. I think this has to do with his attention to detail and his aversion to using modern shortcuts. Here, Stephen takes us through the pre-planning phase of a custom cabinetry project.

Custom bookshelves—designed by architect Carlos Huber, built by Stephen—in my former NYC apartment.

STEPHEN FANUKA

FOUR STEPS TO GETTING STARTED:

STEP 1: GATHER INSPIRATION. Do you want traditional or contemporary cabinetry? Will it be painted or stained? Find photos to help you develop a vision that you can clearly communicate—that's our starting point.

STEP 2: TAKE MEASUREMENTS. How much wall space do you have to work with? What are the dimensions of the items you want to store inside the cabinets?

STEP 3: FIND YOUR CABINETMAKER. Ask neighbors or get a recommendation from your architect or interior designer, if you are working with someone. It's a red flag if the person you reach out to takes a week to return your phone call or if their proposal seems unprofessional. This is a long process; good communication is vital.

STEP 4: APPROVE YOUR DESIGN. Your cabinetmaker should create a shop drawing, which is essentially a blueprint, that includes the front and side elevations of the design. A good contractor will talk through the plans with you.

OTHER CONSIDERATIONS:

LOOK AT WOOD SAMPLES BEFORE MAKING A DECISION. Take them home and see how the light works with them. The same goes for paint colors, if you are planning to paint your cabinetry.

MAKE A NOTE OF YOUR FINAL PAINT FINISH OR STAIN SELECTION. In ten years' time, you won't have a clue what it was. You can easily touch up high-quality cabinets, but obviously you have to get the color right.

THERE'S NO POINT IN TRYING TO UPGRADE INEXPENSIVE CABINETS. But if you have old, quality cupboards, they are worth refinishing. I'm also all for reusing hardware, because it can be so expensive.

AVOID PARTICLE BOARD. It warps, it's cheap, and it is basically made from glued-together, heated-up sawdust. In my shop, we use solid wood or three-quarter-inch plywood with veneer.

HONESTY AND INTEGRITY ARE EVERYTHING. I had a customer tell me: "You charged me for a Mercedes. You gave me a Mercedes." I believe in giving people what they've paid for, and you should make sure whoever you work with believes the same.

STYLING GUIDE

THE BOOKSHELF

My process for styling a bookshelf always starts the same way, with piles of books and objects all over the floor. I haven't found a way without first making a mess. Figuring out which things look good together is trial and error. You have to keep trying different combinations and placements until you find the right balance. It's best to edit each shelf, one at a time, and then stand back and move entire sections until you get it right overall.

BOOKS DON'T ALWAYS NEED TO BE STANDING UP. Rest them on their sides, and arrange objects on top.

I SORT BOOKS BY COVER COLOR, NOT SUBJECT. I know this is controversial, but I prefer seeing them that way; it's less visually chaotic.

GATHER A DIVERSE MIX OF OBJECTS, and look for variety in shape, size, and material.

VARY THE CONTENTS OF YOUR GROUPINGS. If one arrangement is book heavy, the next one should have more objects. Keep standing back and taking in the whole picture until the balance feels right.

HANG SOMETHING ON THE BACK WALL OF THE BOOKCASE: This gives your arrangement depth.

ORIGIN STORIES

The collection of necklaces on the wall is something we started as a family. They hang from an old brass soap dish attached to the wall with a piece of coral sitting on top.

LIGHTING A FAMILY ROOM

The first thing to consider when selecting lighting is the natural light that already exists. What does the space feel like at sunrise, mid-morning, late afternoon, after the sun sets? I like to bring in different types of lighting because variety allows you to control mood.

Also think about the activities you will do in this space, all of which might need their own lighting source. If you want a reading nook, for instance, it should have a floor lamp or an adjustable sconce. If you like to watch movies in complete darkness, I would suggest lamps with low-watt bulbs or a dimmer. Overhead fixtures should never be your only source of light in any room, especially in a space with multiple uses.

It's important that architecture and the features of a room don't disappear once the ceiling lights are off. In this Palm Springs, California, family room, we included a set of sconces flanking a custom built-in and low table lamps behind a leather floor screen to draw attention to these moments.

Jean Royère
FRANK

THE MOMENTS

THAT MAKE THE ROOM

FIND SPACE FOR MULTIUSE SEATING: A pair of stools or a bench that can be moved around the room as needed, a daybed that holds three people sitting or one person napping. The versatility of these pieces help this room to function well.

GO HEAVY ON FRAMED FAMILY PHOTOS. This is the place for them. It makes everyone smile to look around and see themselves represented at different stages of their lives. I have pictures of my mom when she was a baby in our family room, and photos of Jeremiah and me when we had just met. Our kids love to hear the stories behind each picture, to connect to great-grandparents or family they were never able to meet.

MAKE THE FLOOR AS COMFORTABLE AS POSSIBLE. Anticipate that people might end up sitting on the floor, that kids and their friends will be playing there, so both durability and softness matter.

USE SATURATED COLORS AND TIGHTLY WOVEN TEXTILES; both will hide daily wear. We covered the walls of this NYC family room in a rich, olive-green wool, and repeated the same fabric on the dining chairs. The finish will only get better with age.

ENTRIES

One of my all-time favorite rooms is the entry of our NYC apartment. When I walk through the front door, I am welcomed by some of our best design ideas—the 200-year-old stone table that sat outside for one hundred of those years, a modern painting by Simon Mathers in contrast with the classic architectural mouldings. I've always loved a home that unfolds, revealing itself gradually as you move through it. The entry is the starting point, an important introduction to the language of your home. With that in mind, here are some suggestions, so you can start thinking about your own space:

- Lighting should have character and personality. Consider an old lantern, something sculptural from the 1960s, or a fixture that introduces a new material.
- Take some risks. Use an object that belongs outside inside, or add something very formal, like an ornately carved mirror, even if the space feels casual. Play with contrast.
- Reach for your dream architectural materials, especially if you have a small space. The labor costs for installing a stone floor are usually the same, whether the tiles are spectacular or not.

When Jeremiah and I decided to update our entry, we replaced the stone floor with antique Spanish stone from Paris Ceramics. We left the existing limestone border, which saved us both time and money.

WHATEVER YOU DO, PLEASE DON'T . . .

- **AVOID DEFINING THIS SPACE**—even if, technically, it is not a proper room. This is easier than you might think. (See page 166.)
- **SKIP THE PART WHERE YOU CREATE SMART, CONCEALED, AND HANDSOME STORAGE SOLUTIONS.** A pile of shoes should not be the moment that welcomes you home, but a woven basket that hides them could be.
- **OVERLOOK AN OPPORTUNITY TO INCLUDE A PERSONAL TOUCH.** A framed photo; a small, cherished painting; or a meaningful object creates warmth and familiarity.

ABOVE: When you don't have a defined entryway, give the eye a place to land: a console under a painting or a chest of drawers with a mirror above and a pair of lamps for symmetry. I like to include something unexpected, like this modern architectural chair.

OPPOSITE: Our clients asked for an entry that felt cozy and welcoming, something that is not easily achieved in a space with soaring ceilings. We placed a large round table in the center of the room, and hung a vintage, Italian pendant above it, which did two things simultaneously: it brought the eye down to focus on the furniture, and centered the room, creating a more intimate moment.

STYLE VS. STUFF

I don't like to see a lot of *stuff* in an entry. Shoes, mail, keys, bags, coats—none of these items make a great first impression to your home. There are beautiful ways of keeping essentials easily accessible but also out of sight.

An extremely organized coat closet is an ideal solution. Swapping out a single hanging bar for two—one hung high in the closet, the other halfway down—doubles your storage. Consider adding vintage hooks to the wall or the back of the door, or tiered shoe storage along the bottom, to help get everything off the floor.

When an entry does *not* have a closet the first thing I look for is the space to add one. Can I steal two feet from an adjacent room to construct a closet to house everything the family needs? It is always a worthwhile investment.

If a coat closet is not an option, furniture can help you decorate around the issue. Armoires or chests of drawers can go a long way in keeping this zone decluttered.

---

1. **A BEAUTIFUL, CARVED ARMOIRE** is a great substitute for a closet. Replace all or some of the shelves with a hanging rod.
2. **AN EXTRA-DEEP, STROLLER-FRIENDLY CLOSET**, seen on the far right side of this entry, makes a lot of sense if you have young kids. Pay attention to the width of the closet door if you are renovating; it should be wide enough that a stroller or luggage (when you no longer need all the things that children require) can easily roll in and out.
3. **FRAMELESS JIB DOORS** don't interrupt the flow of the space, which makes the footprint of your entry feel larger and gives you the storage you need. (If you're not familiar with a jib door, turn to page 262.)
4. **A VINTAGE SEMAINIER** is a tall chest with seven drawers, one for each day of the week. These pieces take up very little space but are a great storage solution.

1

2

3

4

MAKING AN ENTRANCE

Every house has its own architectural challenges. Homes without a defined entry. Entries so enormous the owners would rather use a side door. Whatever the design dilemma, I always ask myself the same question: How can I define the space and create a moment that feels both special and welcoming?

The square footage of an entry is often small enough to put more expensive building materials within reach. In our former townhouse, Jeremiah and I added a pair of salvaged French metal doors that framed the tiny space (see page 70). I love intricate flooring, whether you paint a pattern on existing wood or invest in stone that already has a lot of patina. Wall treatments—like natural woven grasscloth or antique mirrored tiles, or even a warm paint color—add a personal touch.

LEFT: To keep her entry from feeling too formal, my design partner, Lauren, brought in a bleached French chest of drawers from the 1940s, previously used as her daughter's changing table. It isn't grandiose by intention, instead it reads rustic, warm, unpretentious, and welcoming.

OPPOSITE: This foyer on the Upper East Side of Manhattan is the connective tissue of the home, so we gave it its own identity with modern photography, ceiling mouldings, and a detailed stone border on the floor that felt separate from the rooms around it.

THE MOMENTS

THAT MAKE THE ROOM

RECLAIMED STONE FLOORS ARE BEAUTIFUL BUT NOT PRECIOUS. They are already chipped and well worn. There's no amount of snow on the bottom of your kid's shoes that can destroy them. This material is elegant but durable.

USE HISTORICAL REFERENCES FOR FLOORING INSPIRATION. If you study photos of old Roman homes or Venetian palazzos, you will find interesting, unexpected color combinations (rose with black, terracotta and ecru) and bold geometric patterns. Somehow they still feel decidedly modern.

THE FURNITURE SHOULD CONTRAST THE ARCHITECTURE OF THE ROOM. If you have traditional architecture, for example, reach for modern pieces. Pairing opposites in this way highlights the best aspects of both.

MAKE SPACE FOR SOMETHING LIVING. A natural element softens the transition from the outdoors in: fresh-cut flowers on the center table; tall branches in an oversized vase; or, as we did in our home, an eight-foot olive tree in an ancient stone pot (see page 161).

MY BEST ADVICE ON WHERE TO SPEND & WHERE TO SAVE

SPEND ON . . .

- Wallcoverings
- A console or chest of drawers
- Special flooring
- An interesting ceiling fixture
- A vintage mirror

SAVE ON . . .

- Small vintage accessories you can find locally
- Woven baskets or other handsome storage solutions
- Drawer organizers
- Flowers or branches
- Skip the rug in here

KITCHENS

I spend a lot of time in our kitchen, and practically none of that time is spent cooking. This isn't the book to learn about uber-efficient work triangle theory or ideal appliance distances. What I can tell you is that this room, where we gather 90 percent of the time, is an opportunity to be as inventive and personal as any other in your home, without sacrificing function. For me, a kitchen is not only about the finishes you select but how your true style shows up in those choices. Here are some of my favorite ways to personalize a kitchen:

- Create a lighting plan that is practical and includes a combination of vintage and new fixtures.
- Bring in details that most would not consider in this room, like small lamps on the countertop, framed photos, or groupings of pottery.
- Choose a mix of finishes: stones, ceramics, metals, woods (both painted and natural).
- Pick a moment to be adventurous. Is it the color of the cabinetry? The shape of the range hood?

A bold backsplash is a great place to make a statement; it brings so much personality to the room.

WHATEVER YOU DO, PLEASE DON'T . . .

- **BE AFRAID TO MAKE DEEPLY PERSONAL DESIGN CHOICES.** If a busy, veined marble is your dream, make it reality.
- **LET TRENDS SWAY YOU, ESPECIALLY WHEN SELECTING BUILT-IN FINISHES.** A trend-driven kitchen is a kitchen with an expiration date.
- **BUY BARGAIN APPLIANCES.** It doesn't matter how handsome your cabinet hardware is if you can't count on your oven to work.

LIGHTING A KITCHEN

Overhead fixtures are essential, but they shouldn't be your only source of lighting. There are other more beautiful and often more affordable ways to have lighting that also functions well. Our kitchen has one ceiling fixture (a vintage Italian pendant by Lumi) with six exposed bulbs—enough to flood the entire room with the light we need. We added painted gallery lights to the cabinets, and a pair of wall sconces flanking the sink. Three table lamps on the countertops create a soft glow in the evening. We change the lighting depending on the time of day, the amount of natural light, and what we are doing at any particular moment. Breakfast around the island is flooded by sunlight. Making dinner requires the overhead fixture and cabinet lights. Sneaking in after bedtime to eat the last cookie is lit by a small table lamp.

FOLLOWING PAGE: It's second nature for me to turn off the main lights before bed, but leave a small lamp on overnight.

LET'S TALK ABOUT CABINETS

Cabinet style dictates the style of your kitchen, full stop. Despite the intimidating number of options, there are really only two main choices: a flat panel, which takes you in a modern direction, or a recessed panel, which is more traditional. (The latter includes any type of Shaker, modified Shaker, beaded detail, etc.) Pick a direction so you can focus on the more fun design decisions. Do you want painted cabinets or stained wood? How do you feel about using another material in some of the doors: wavy glass, aged mirror, woven metal mesh? What kind of hardware and finishes speak to you? These are the details that will bring your style into this space, so your kitchen can feel custom, even if most of the materials are not. (For ideas on hardware, turn to page 388.)

1. **GLASS-FRONT DOORS** with exposed, aged brass cremones make a newly renovated kitchen feel 150 years old.
2. **RAISED PANEL CABINETS** with decorative iron pulls are a classic option for traditionalists.
3. **CABINET DOORS INSET WITH WOVEN METAL MESH** let you display objects and are a timeless choice.
4. **PANEL-READY APPLIANCES** allow you to have a seamless look.

1
2
3
4

THE ARTISTRY OF STONE

As you walk through a stone showroom it is easy to forget that the polished slabs you are viewing are a material with a long history, that artisans have been chiseling away at stone, creating detailed architectural components for over three centuries. Picking your stone slab is the first—but not the only—decision you should make for your counters and backsplash. Think about how you might highlight the material's sculptural potential. For a backsplash, could it be shaped or capped with a small ledge to display objects? What profiles and edge details would make your kitchen island even more special? Be thoughtful about the finishing details.

1

2

3

4

FOUR STONE DETAILS TO CONSIDER. . .

1. A stepped backsplash feels important over the sink and oven.

2. A handsome shelf above the stove, made from leftover material.

3. Angled drainage grooves to keep water from pooling on the countertop.

4. A deep ledge behind the oven lined with a mix of decorative objects and cooking oils.

A GUIDE TO COUNTERTOP EDGE DETAILS

Double demi bullnose edge

Brass-wrapped eased edge

When I want to create something special with stone in a kitchen, I start by researching the marble fountains in European cathedrals and Roman bathhouses. It may seem incredibly specific, but these references are where I find some of my best ideas. A single countertop edge profile is common, but I like to use more than one: a decorative edge detail on an island with something simple everywhere else.

Ogee bullnose edge

French coved edge

ANOTHER THING . . .

Counter edge style names vary by fabricator. If you are considering one of these decorative details, give your contractor an image of the look you are hoping to achieve.

In this Los Angeles kitchen, we installed an eighteenth-century limestone fireplace surround over the stove to anchor the space.

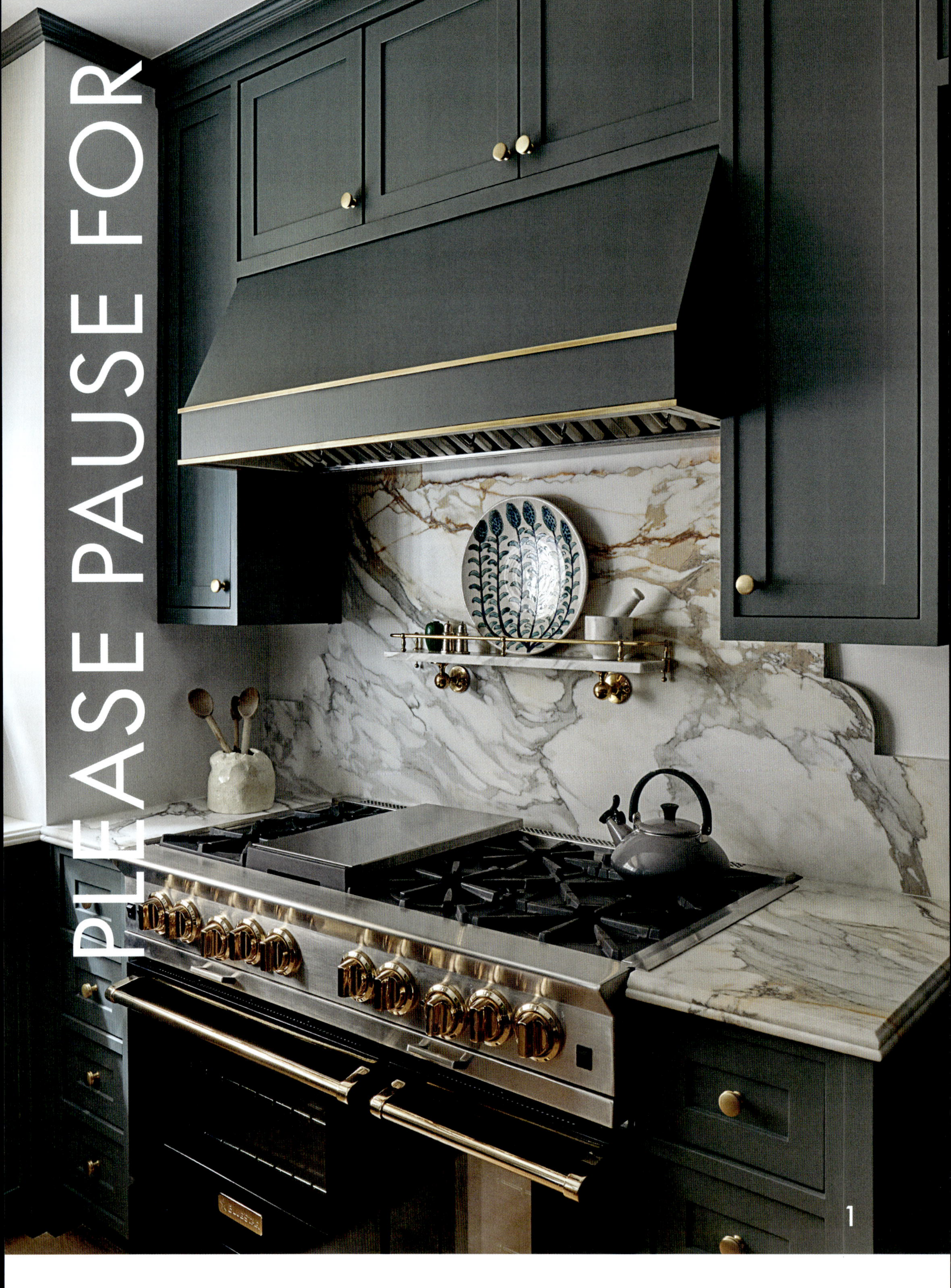
PLEASE PAUSE FOR
1

RANGE HOODS

Proper ventilation is essential in a kitchen, and functionality should be the priority. I gravitate to timeless options, like cladding the hood in stone or clean drywall with a decorative trim. Here are a few more treatments to consider.

---

1. **BLEND IN WITH THE CABINETS.** Color-match the hood to make it less prominent.
2. **USE SIMPLE DRYWALL.** I like to trim the edge in the same type of stone as the countertop.
3. **BUY THE SET.** This hood and range create a handsome, industrial feel in the kitchen.

EVERYONE LOVES A COFFEE STATION

Most of us don't care where our first cup of coffee comes from as long as it makes it into our hands almost immediately after we wake up. There is a lot to be said, however, for taking an essential part of your morning routine and giving it its own beautiful destination: Using a cup you really enjoy holding; storing coffee beans or loose tea in elegant containers; sitting down, even for five minutes, to enjoy the moment. A dedicated coffee station—or even a beautifully styled tray on your counter that has everything you need—creates a ceremony and starts your day in the right frame of mind.

WHERE TO SET ONE UP . . .

1. **STEPS AWAY FROM THE BED.** Lauren's coffee station is in an area just off her bedroom and includes an 18-inch dishwasher, because, as she says, "I wasn't messing around."

2. **INSIDE A PIECE OF FURNITURE.** Our coffee equipment lives in one of the cabinets in our dining room. We used leftover marble on the bottom shelf so it would be easy to clean.

3. **IN A SMALL AREA IN YOUR KITCHEN** where you can keep all that you need in the morning on display.

2

3

THE GALLEY KITCHEN

The easiest way to design a galley kitchen is to work with a tight material and color palette. If you can, try to add a small space to sit—counter stools or a café table and two chairs. This creates a moment to enjoy yourself in a space often only ruled by function.

1. Always extend cabinets to the ceiling regardless of the size of your kitchen. It makes the room feel larger.
2. Invest in details that feel impactful. Lauren painted the doors and windows black and hung an antique lantern in the eating area of her former kitchen; your eye skips straight to these details.
3. A small kitchen is another opportunity to reach for high-end finishes, like your dream stone countertops, that would be cost prohibitive in a bigger space.

1

2

3

FOUR TIMELESS KITCHEN DESIGNS

From dark and moody to classic with European influences, these kitchens are some of my firm's most asked about designs. It is the details that make them special, so I am sharing those here with a list of resources. The most beautiful kitchens are the ones that reflect the people who live in them everyday, so please think of these recommendations as *more* inspiration to take what you love but make them your own.

RICH AND CLASSIC

GET THE LOOK

1. **CABINET PULLS:** Founders Pulls in unlacquered brass, Classic Brass.
2. **ISLAND:** Custom aged brass.
3. **STONE:** Calacatta Macchia Vecchia, ABC Stone.
4. **CABINET KNOBS:** Chautauqua Knobs in unlacquered brass, Classic Brass.
5. **CABINETS:** Painted Shaker.
6. **PAINT COLOR:** Nitty Gritty, Portola Paints.

OLD WORLD CHARM

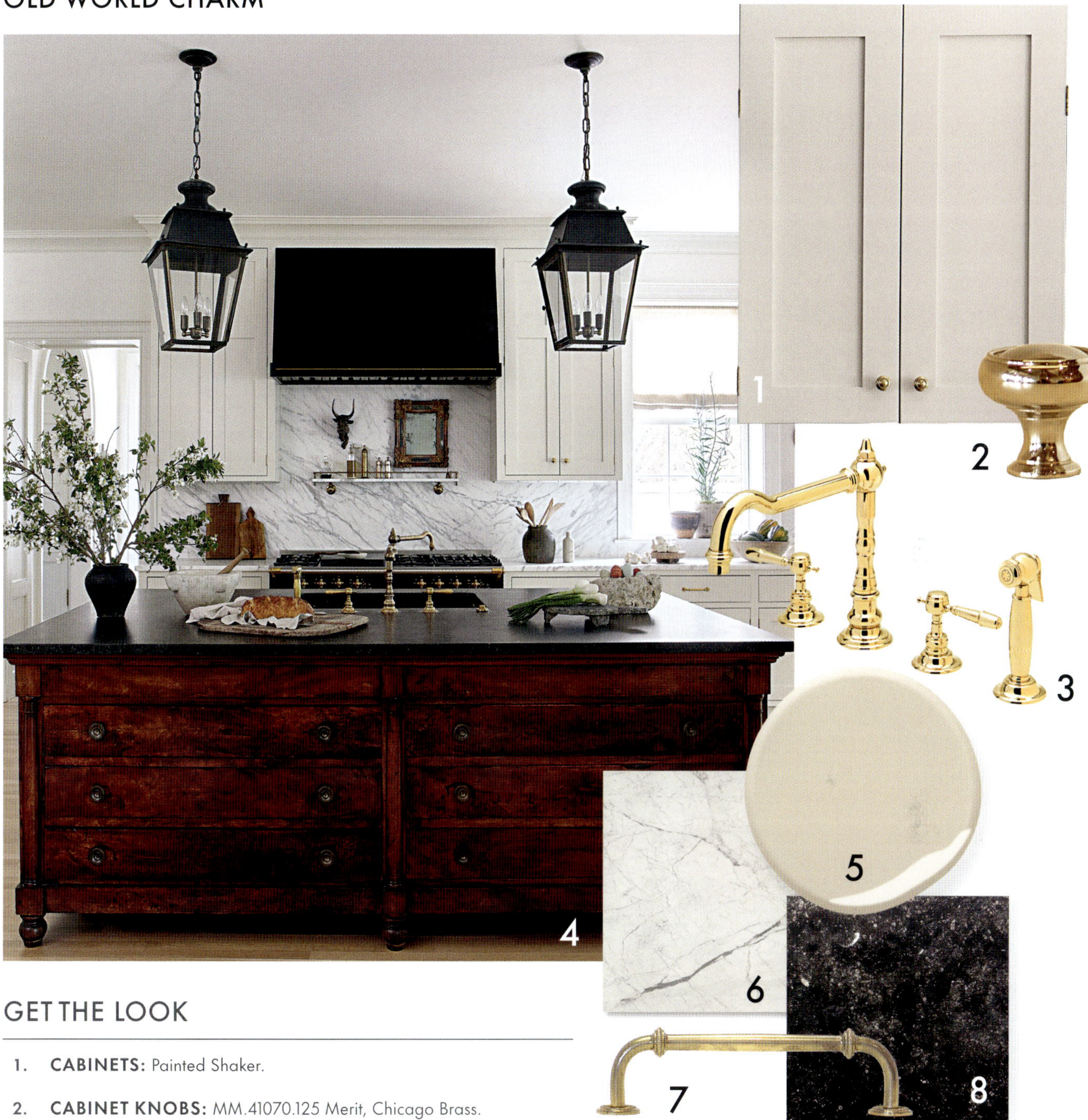

GET THE LOOK

1. **CABINETS:** Painted Shaker.
2. **CABINET KNOBS:** MM.41070.125 Merit, Chicago Brass.
3. **FAUCET:** Julia Three-hole Faucet with sprayer, Waterworks.
4. **ISLAND:** An old French storefront counter retrofitted by Old Plank Antiques in Chicago.
5. **PAINT COLOR:** Shaded White, Farrow & Ball.
6. **STONE ON PERIMETER CABINETS:** Statuary Marble, Calia Stone.
7. **CABINET PULLS:** Bronzes de France Pulls with Rosettes, Chicago Brass.
8. **STONE ON THE ISLAND:** Petit Granit.

WARM AND MODERN

GET THE LOOK

1. **CABINET KNOBS:** Egg Knobs in dark bronze, Rocky Mountain Hardware.
2. **CABINETS:** Flat panel in white oak.
3. **STONE:** Calacatta Paonazzo, Unique Stone Imports.
4. **CABINET PULLS:** Rail Pulls in dark bronze, Rocky Mountain Hardware.

GET THE LOOK

1. **CABINET KNOBS:** European Iron Cabinet Knob and Backplate, Whitechapel.
2. **CABINETS:** Painted raised panel.
3. **FAUCET:** Custom bronze, Van Cronenburg.
4. **PAINT COLOR:** Saint Sauvant, Portola Paints.
5. **STONE:** Calacatta Paonazzo, ABC Stone.

THE MOMENTS

THAT MAKE THE ROOM

CONSIDER FURNITURE AS A STORAGE SOLUTION. An antique chest of drawers brings warmth and imperfections to a kitchen with newly painted cabinets. When Lauren was planning her island, her father, an antiques dealer, came up with the idea of using an old French storefront counter as the base. They found one at auction, and he retrofit it for plumbing and added the new granite top.

ADD AN OPEN SHELF TO THE BACKSPLASH, and use it for more than oils and spices. Bring in decorative objects that introduce another material or era. In our kitchen in Los Angeles, we hung an old mirror off-center above the stove. When it comes to styling, try not to overthink it.

A CURTAIN BREAKS THE MONOTONY OF CABINET DOORS. It is an old design trick found in rustic kitchens for years; the modern interpretations use elevated materials like heavy Belgian linen. Making one is simple: You need a panel of fabric gathered at the top, weighted at the bottom, then slid onto a metal rod.

AN OLD PAINTING OR MODERN PHOTOGRAPH IN A BEAUTIFUL FRAME IS UNEXPECTED. I like when a room has a sense of discovery. Something framed is a place for the eye to land as it travels through the space.

MY BEST ADVICE ON WHERE TO SPEND & WHERE TO SAVE

SPEND ON . . .

- Appliances
- Plumbing fixtures
- Hardware
- Countertops
- Range hoods

SAVE ON . . .

- Lighting
- Cabinetry (some ready-made options work really well)
- Decorative accessories
- Glasses and dishes
- Small decorative rugs
- Counter stools

DINING SPACES

Should a dining room *always* be formal? The answer is no. It is more important, I think, that a dining room is *used*. If you entertain frequently and prefer the table set with your best silver, then it should feel grand and elevated. But if you are not a particularly formal person and your dining room sits untouched for most of the year, it's a missed opportunity to enjoy all of the rooms in your home. Eating in the dining room should not feel like an effort. If it does, consider taking the formality down a bit. Could you swap out the chairs for a more casual, upholstered option? Could you add a small settee or banquette on one side? It is simple to dress up a table on special occasions with a pair of candlesticks and a set of embroidered napkins, but it is hard to take the rigidity out of a room designed only for formal entertaining. Here are some ideas for creating a space that's beautiful that you can enjoy every day:

- Decide on the correct level of comfort based on how you dine and entertain. (Turn to page 200 for advice.)
- Add a reflective surface, such as a gilded mirror, for charm.
- Consider what happens after dinner. Do you stay around the table? Would you rather move around the room? Can you add spaces for those moments into your furniture plan?
- Look for fabrics that are dark or have a small pattern, which will hide wear more effectively.

This eat-in kitchen nook in Chicago is a reminder that casual dining spaces can feel tailored and handsome.

WHATEVER YOU DO, PLEASE DON'T . . .

- **BUY DINING CHAIRS WITHOUT SITTING IN THEM FIRST.** Uncomfortable seating is almost worse than bad food.
- **OVERLOOK STORAGE OPPORTUNITIES**—or places to display serving pieces and tableware.
- **LET EVERYTHING BE THE SAME HEIGHT.** Add a taller piece of furniture, or hang a large painting or mirror, to direct the eye up.

LIGHTING A DINING ROOM

Consider candles. As much as I appreciate a statement fixture above the table, before I make any lighting selections, I stop and think about how they will play with candlelight. We light candles in our home every night, whether it's a family dinner or takeout with friends, a small gesture that elevates any meal. Putting every fixture on a dimmer and adding wall sconces will help you control the mood; the sconces wash the walls in a soft light, while the glow of candles warms the table.

These hand-blown Murano glass fixtures from Studio Glustin deflect a magical light around the room.

TABLE SHAPE: ROUND VS. RECTANGULAR

CONSIDER A ROUND (OR OVAL) TABLE IF . . .

- You like dinner parties to be low-key and intimate.
- You prefer a seating arrangement that feels casual.
- You want to break up the lines of a rectangular room.

CONSIDER A RECTANGULAR TABLE IF . . .

- Your gatherings are more formal.
- You need to seat a large number of people (in which case, look for options with additional leaves).
- You prefer a seating arrangement where separate groups can be conversing at the same time.
- Your dining room is narrow

CREATING ATMOSPHERE

There are certain questions to consider in a dining room. How many people do you want to seat? What is your everyday number, and what is the maximum? Do you use placemats or tablecloths?

I also like to land on a mood. When Jeremiah and I were designing our dining room, we wanted people to feel elevated and as welcome as possible. The architectural features already set a formal tone: the elaborate moulding, the herringbone floors, the hand-cut vintage mirror tiles. So we were more loose with where we placed the furniture, a built-in bench on one side of the table, a row of vintage French leather chairs on the other. The finishes our guests interact with aren't precious. The chairs are wipeable. A glass without a coaster isn't going to hurt the stone tabletop. The room *looks* elevated, but *lives* casual.

I have always admired Aerin Lauder's easy elegance, her approach to entertaining and life. She was raised on the Upper East Side of Manhattan, knowing all the rules of how to do things properly: set a table, host a party. She took that information and decided what worked for her family and what did not. Her lifestyle brand, AERIN, is a good indicator of how it all shook out. The way she pulls from different inspirations for a table setting—old and new, formal and casual—feels effortless, like she breezed through the room, and it came together in minutes. But thirty years of decorating has taught me that it takes a lot of preplanning for a moment to look unplanned. Here are Aerin's tips for setting a beautiful, effortless-*looking* table.

AERIN LAUDER

FRESH FLOWERS ARE ESSENTIAL. Use them as a jumping-off point for your color scheme.

MARK THE SEASONS WITH YOUR FLOWER CHOICES. I use lilacs in spring and deep, rich red tones in the fall. Although you can get almost any variety of flower year-round, it is nice when what is happening on your table reflects what is blooming in your garden.

MAKE SURE YOUR CENTERPIECE ISN'T TOO HIGH. My mother taught me that. There is nothing more obstructive to conversation than a huge flower arrangement people can't see over.

FIND INSPIRATION FOR YOUR TABLE IN TRAVEL AND FRIENDSHIP. I pick up so many ideas from the places I visit, from books, and from friends' homes. I also love Willow Crossley, a wonderful florist in the English countryside. I follow her on Instagram and feel so inspired by her tablescapes.

MIX HEIRLOOMS WITH NEW TREASURES. That is the secret to a memorable table setting. I love using wonderful pieces that were handed down to me by my grandmother, Estée [Lauder], with objects found on my travels.

DON'T *ONLY* USE YOUR NICE SILVER AND CRYSTAL ON SPECIAL OCCASIONS. If we are having takeout at home, there will still be candles on the table, cloth napkins, and pretty silver spoons to serve the food. I love that contrast.

ALWAYS HAVE ASSIGNED SEATING FOR SIX OR MORE GUESTS. My evening becomes more special if I sit next to someone I have never met before and learn something new. Even if it is a family event, I still like to have a seating plan.

A SMALL GIFT IS A THOUGHTFUL GESTURE. I sometimes put a fragrance, or some other little present, at each person's seat when hosting a dinner party or luncheon, a wonderful little tradition established by my grandmother.

This NYC dining space belongs to a family with older kids. It has seating that can shrink or expand depending on who is making it home for dinner that night, and how many friends are coming with them.

SOME SOUND SHOPPING ADVICE

When shopping for dining chairs, it is important to consider the design from the back as well as the front. What will they look like around your table? Here are some other factors to think about as you make your decision:

- Decide on a level of comfort. Armless and high-backed chairs are more formal. Something fully upholstered feels casual and approachable.
- Play with opposites. Intricate chairs paired with a simple table or vice versa.
- Don't be afraid to mix it up. An upholstered banquette or bench across from architectural chairs, or something very structured with something soft is a more casual way to dine that works for dinner parties and Sunday morning breakfast.
- Choose between arms or no arms. The latter allows you to fit more people around the table.
- Keep an extra pair of chairs on standby. You can pull them to the table for large gatherings.
- Vintage chairs are always a good choice. If you need more than four, search for multiple smaller sets (that are similar *enough* to one another). This is often more cost-effective than buying a group of eight or twelve.

CARVING OUT A BREAKFAST AREA

Having a casual spot for quick bites or homework sessions in the kitchen becomes a natural hub for your family. A banquette against the wall feels clean and sophisticated, and somehow always has the space to accommodate one more person. Take the time to consider storage; deep drawers under a bench are a good place to stash large serving pieces or rarely used appliances and cookware.

A STATEMENT LIGHT IS IMPORTANT. Define this area with a ceiling fixture.

REALITY CHECK

LIVING WITH KIDS

Food will drop. Drinks will spill. If you have anyone under the age of ten in your home, you likely encounter any number of mystery substances daily. Here are a few suggestions for getting ahead of the inevitable "sorrys."

- Leather is a good idea. It's wipeable, wears well, and looks even better worn in over time.
- Dark fabrics with a pattern or tight weave help to hide everyday wear and tear.
- A banquette in an outdoor fabric is easier to maintain.
- A vintage wooden table means you don't have to worry about marks, scratches, and stains; they can only add to the patina.
- Dense stones like slate or bluestone are practically indestructible.

A PEDESTAL TABLE IS THE ONLY OPTION. More people can fit around it, and it is easier to navigate when sliding in and out of a banquette.

EVERYONE LOVES A HOME BAR

I enjoy the ceremony of making a cocktail. Offering a guest a drink feels gracious and personal, a few minutes to connect with them before the evening gets started. Whether you have a built-in bar, a cart, a dedicated space on the counter, or an armoire you have outfitted for this purpose, styling a bar works best when you do the following:

- Keep everything you need within arm's reach: the liquor, the glassware, a cocktail spoon, ice.
- Add a small vintage lamp to light the area when the overhead fixture is dimmed.
- Mix in personal styling moments—art or framed photographs, pottery, or a vintage candlestick.

CAN YOU CREATE A BAR . . .

1. **AS ITS OWN, DESIGNATED ROOM?** For a joint design project in Montecito, California, Jeremiah and I turned a small space off the main living area into a lounge with a custom bar on one wall.
2. **INSIDE A CONVERTED ARMOIRE?** We retrofitted an antique wardrobe with a wet bar for our clients in Lake Forest, Illinois.
3. **INSIDE A CABINET?** Everything we need for drinks is kept on the shelves of this vintage cabinet in our living room. For parties, I move what I need to the kitchen counter, but leave the doors open, so guests can help themselves.
4. **ON YOUR COUNTER?** Arrange a collection of your favorite spirits and mixers on a cutting board or tray so it feels contained and edited.

1

2

Tito's
Handmade
VODKA
ASTRAL
Moscow
Mule
MARGARITA
3

TRUFF
4

THE DESIGN FOR LAUREN'S BAR BEGAN WITH HER DREAM FLOOR. The rust and cream stone tile set the mood, while the other details—the stripped beams, the alabaster light fixtures—were chosen to ensure that all the elements in the space brought character and charm.

LOCATION IS EVERYTHING. My firm designed a custom wall unit for clients in Chicago that sits at an intersection of three main traffic points. On one side is the living room, on the other is the dining room, and directly in front are doors that lead to the pool.

Until the late 1800s, people dined by candlelight out of necessity, not out of ceremony. If you study dining rooms from that time, they always included reflective surfaces. The more mirrors, the more light, as the glow from the candles was reflected over and over.

THE MOMENTS

THAT MAKE THE ROOM

KEEP YOUR BEST PIECES IN THE DINING ROOM. Setting the table is a creative outlet for me; my contribution to the dinner party because I can't cook. Having what I own easily accessible takes away the stress of running around looking for a platter as friends are ringing the doorbell.

FIND SPACE TO INTRODUCE ANOTHER SURFACE—a sideboard, a small round table in a corner, a chest of drawers, or a console. It is an extra spot for candles, florals, or serving dessert.

INVEST IN SMART STORAGE. When space is limited, a shallow cabinet—with a minimum depth of five inches—can hold all the things you need for entertaining.

CONSIDER WHAT HAPPENS AFTER DINNER IS DONE. Another place to land—a window seat or chairs around a small table—gives people somewhere to move to when it's time for coffee and tea to be served.

MY BEST ADVICE ON WHERE TO SPEND & WHERE TO SAVE

SPEND ON . . .

- The table
- Interesting chairs you love
- Statement lighting
- A mirror or reflective surface
- Textiles that will wear well and hold up to stains

SAVE ON . . .

- A pair of great candleholders
- Vases for flowers
- Serving pieces
- Clear glassware
- Placemats
- Cloth napkins

6 ROOMS TO RESET

Bedrooms | The Spaces in Between
Bathrooms | Powder Rooms

BEDROOMS

My younger brother and I shared a bedroom for most of my childhood. Even then, the Virgo in me couldn't handle the laundry that spread from his side of the room into mine. At thirteen, what I wanted most in the world was my own room. I think this is one reason why I approach bedrooms as serene and organized spaces. I like having framed photos on a table, and fresh flowers by the bed. Not huge investments, but investments in thoughtfulness. This space is the last place you encounter before going to sleep, and the first place that greets you in the morning. How you feel in it matters. Here are some ways to ensure yours is making the right impression on you:

- Look for storage solutions that are as beautiful as they are functional: decorative boxes to hide remotes or silver trays to hold jewelry.
- Layer bedding to feel interesting and collected, not perfectly matched. Crisp white sheets, a woven blanket, and throw pillows made from textiles you love will always look great.
- Plan for a variety of lighting that includes something dimmable overhead and table lamps or sconces by the bed.
- Include somewhere to sit besides the bed.

RIGHT: The materials you choose are especially important in this space, where you can set soft layers against the hard finishes. In our NYC bedroom, Jeremiah and I used vintage travertine tables by Samuel Marx next to a long velvet headboard. We paired 1960s Swedish table lamps and a collection of antique silver boxes; a heavy linen coverlet and striped pillows.

PREVIOUS PAGE: A calm bedroom is my favorite place to reset. Having symmetry—pairs of lamps, pairs of bedside tables—creates a sense of balance and ease.

WHATEVER YOU DO, PLEASE DON'T . . .

- **BUY A MATTRESS WITHOUT TESTING IT OUT FIRST.** Sleep is too important.
- **USE YOUR BEDROOM AS A CATCHALL.** If end-of-the-day cleanup involves pushing the mess from your public spaces into your private ones, now is the time to find the right storage solution.
- **BUY BADLY MADE SHEETS AND PILLOWS.** Trust your hand. Find what feels right. Then invest in more than one set.

For a shared project in Montecito, California, Jeremiah and I upholstered the bed in a rich burnt sienna fabric. The dark shade in a room of light neutrals immediately catches your eye.

LET'S TALK ABOUT HEADBOARDS

A bedroom feels incomplete without a headboard, even if you are a strict minimalist. All the plush pillows and textural layers need a structured counterpoint. There are a lot of ways a headboard can be a statement. It can be an interesting shape, an exaggerated scale, or a contrasting color. Avoid busy prints; a solid fabric allows you to easily change everything around it without having to reupholster the largest piece of furniture in the room. Here are some ideas that can add focus and a personal touch to your space.

1. **PUNCTUATED PIPING.** The sculptural shape of this mohair-covered headboard is even more pronounced because of the darker trim.

2. **MAKING WAVES.** A smart way to create a sense of movement in a small space, this custom headboard doesn't require a lot of decorative pillows.

3. **A WARM EMBRACE.** The inviting way this bed curves inward defines the intimate space.

4. **EXTRA-EXTRA LONG.** An antique Jean-Michel Frank floor screen positioned behind the upholstered headboard gives the illusion of length.

1

2

3

4

ANOTHER PLACE TO LAND

Consider including a seating area in your bedroom; somewhere you can pack and unpack, have a conversation where one of you is not on the bed. A mini-retreat within your retreat. You will be surprised at how often you find yourself using this space.

1

2

DO YOU HAVE ROOM FOR . . .

1. **A BENCH** at the end of the bed or under a window?
2. **A SIDE CHAIR** next to your bedside table?
3. **A PAIR OF CHAIRS** at the end of the bed?
4. **AN EDITED SEATING ARRANGEMENT,** a small sofa and chairs in a corner?

UP YOUR PILLOW GAME

In the 1980s, when I was a teenager, beds were covered in a half dozen decorative pillows. I don't miss that look. I do love the layers of interest a well thought out combination adds to a room, bringing in patterns and textures and shapes in an unexpected way. So don't be afraid to make a riskier choice here, even if it's the boldest, most expensive fabric in your home.

HOW TO PUT IT ALL TOGETHER . . .

1. **PURPOSELY OFF-KILTER AND RELAXED.** The key here is to make it look casual *and* still have it feel intentional.
2. **THREE IN A ROW, AND ONE TO SPARE.** I prefer when only two pillows are in the same fabric or pattern.
3. **A TRIED-AND-TRUE TRIO.** Take some chances with your fabric choices—a bolder print, a heavier texture, something with needlework.
4. **ONE AND DONE.** An extra-long lumbar pillow is simple and tailored.

This Chicago bedroom is a lovely reminder of why personal spaces take time. The room will evolve as the young couple who lives here add their own objects and cherished heirlooms. If you are starting a project of your own, choose the pieces you need to make the space function first, then relax and enjoy the rest of the process.

WHAT YOU SHOULD KNOW ABOUT BEDSIDE TABLES

Bedside tables are an opportunity to bring special materials into the bedroom, like stone, rattan, metal, or aged wood. Different shapes can make the space feel more dynamic and layered. Consider something antique that introduces another era of design to the mix, even if you don't find a matching pair. Two vintage tables that are similar heights can be an interesting choice. Don't sacrifice surface area to make a statement; this is also an important styling moment.

HOW TO PUT IT ALL TOGETHER . . .

1. **SKIP THE TABLE LAMP** and try a floor lamp or sconce next to the bed.
2. **NATURAL STONE IS A TIMELESS CHOICE**, especially in a room full of rich finishes. This table was made using leftover marble from a recent bathroom renovation.
3. **MAKE STORAGE A PRIORITY,** but make it beautiful, too. This antique Gustavian chest holds it all.
4. **MIX ERAS.** An early twentieth-century alabaster lamp sitting on a Primitive table with a glazed pottery vase and brass bowl feels collected and charming.
5. **A MIDDLE SHELF** is a small-space solution that doubles your surface area.

2

3

4

5

A TELEVISION IN THE BEDROOM

What I'm about to say might be controversial in the design world: I think television in bed is one of life's great pleasures. Jeremiah and I have a TV in our room that we use mostly on the weekends, when the kids want to watch cartoons, or if one of us (me) is home with a pretend flu. What I try *not* to do is have a television be the focal point. Here are some more discreet ideas for its placement.

1. **CONCEAL IT BEHIND DOORS.** In our NYC townhouse, the only place we could fit a small television was over the fireplace. Jeremiah had the idea of using fluted plaster to hide a shallow cabinet above the firebox. (A simpler solution would be to reconfigure an armoire.)

2. **HANG IT TO THE SIDE.** My design partner, Lauren, mounted her television in the corner next to the fireplace, where it is less noticeable when you enter the room.

3. **INSIDE A PIECE OF FURNITURE.** We hid a television in the custom cabinet at the base of this bed, which has a built-in motorized TV lift.

1
2
3

The standard of service at The Carlyle in New York City feels like you've slipped back in time to a more elegant era. It is a classic institution, where you feel welcomed and celebrated. The hotel opened in 1930 and was designed, in part, by Dorothy Draper. Every generation seems to discover and fall in love with this place, and the hotel remains the same—they must be doing something right. Marlene Poynder, the managing director, spoke with me about what it means to be a gracious host, and how to prepare a guest room in your home that feels elevated.

The Carlyle on Manhattan's Upper East Side.

MARLENE POYNDER

A SUBTLE FRAGRANCE SETS A WELCOMING TONE. At The Carlyle, we have a signature scent, which is a lovely mix of citrus and honeysuckle. Create your own with a candle or reed diffuser.

PLACE A MEANINGFUL PHOTO NEXT TO THE BED. If you are hosting a family member, it might be a picture of the two of you when you were both younger. It's a thoughtful touch that instantly makes them feel at home.

WRITE A SHORT WELCOME NOTE, and include important details about your home: alarm codes, Wi-Fi passwords, directions for working the television and thermostat. If it is someone's first time staying with you, give them a quick tour that includes where you keep your plates, glasses, and silverware in the kitchen.

LEARN YOUR GUESTS' LIKES AND DISLIKES. Before they arrive, ask them what they eat and drink, when they go to bed, even what they watch on TV. Having these answers takes some of the guesswork out of hosting.

TRY TO ANTICIPATE THEIR NEEDS. Put plates and pastries out the night before, so they can help themselves to breakfast. It's more relaxing for everyone if they don't have to ask for everything.

MAKE SURE THE BED LOOKS INVITING. Bedrooms can feel intimidating if there are too many hard surfaces and not enough soft ones, or if the bed is overstuffed with decorative pillows. I like an extra blanket draped across the end of the bed and only a few pillows at the head.

HAVE A NICE SET OF GUEST SHEETS. I'm a 400-thread count girl, a side effect of working in luxury hotels for nearly thirty-five years. Your sheets don't have to be expensive, but they do need to be 100 percent cotton or linen—no mixed poly, please.

PROVIDE A CHOICE OF PILLOWS TO SLEEP ON. If you've got feather pillows on the bed, have spare non-down pillows that are a little firmer on hand.

THE MOMENTS
THAT MAKE THE ROOM

BLACKOUT SHADES ARE ESSENTIAL. Carefully weigh design decisions that affect sleep, like choosing the right window treatments. If there is one place in your home to upgrade to something motorized, this is it. Waking up, pressing a button on your bedside table, and having daylight flood in around you is a real luxury.

ADD A READING LIGHT. You will find these in 90 percent of my projects. Task lighting can get overlooked when making lighting choices; they have a reputation for being eyesores. My firm and I have spent a lot of time sourcing handsome options; the one here is by Vaughan Designs.

HAVE SOMETHING LUXURIOUS UNDERFOOT. The bedroom doesn't get as much traffic as other areas of the home, so you can use a rug or carpeting that is a little bit softer, a little bit finer, a little bit lighter. I usually pick natural materials—wool, cotton, linen blend, mohair blend—which are surprisingly easy to clean and last longer than something synthetic.

WARM UP THE WALLS. Whether you use a textured wallcovering or a paper-backed fabric, even an antique tapestry hanging behind the bed (see page 25), adding some depth and richness in this space is always a good move.

MY BEST ADVICE ON WHERE TO SPEND & WHERE TO SAVE

SPEND ON . . .

- A ceiling fixture
- Bedside lamps or sconces
- Custom drapery and shades
- A quality mattress
- Antique or vintage picture frames (for your dresser and bedside table)
- Bedside tables
- A textured wall treatment

SAVE ON . . .

- An upholstered headboard
- Bedding (shop around for the best deals)
- Decorative throws and pillows
- Vintage accessories (visit the flea market)

THE SPACES IN BETWEEN

What do you see when you turn a corner? When you reach the top of the stairs? When you walk down the hallway? Most people don't put a lot of effort into these areas. But historically, if you look at photos of inspiring residences—C. Z. Guest's Templeton estate, the Hôtel de Noailles in Paris—attention to detail in these in-between spaces are what make a home feel "done." On your list of priorities, they often come last. If you've reached the point where you feel good about what you've designed everywhere else, then it's time to look at some of these secondary spaces. This is an opportunity to create something impactful with only a few pieces.

THE LANDING. There have been a hundred iterations of furniture in this space, but what Lauren ultimately decided it needed was a comfortable place to sit, and an interesting mix of accessories that made her happy when she opened her bedroom door every morning.

2

1

OTHER IN-BETWEEN SPACES THAT DESERVE YOUR ATTENTION . . .

1. **THE SIGHT LINES AS YOU TURN A CORNER.** A simple vintage portrait leaning on a marble shelf in the kitchen is where your eye lands as you move from one living space to the next in this NYC apartment.

2. **THE END OF THE HALL** is another place to use furniture you might already own. An arrangement of well-loved vintage pieces works well in this small area at the top of the stairs.

3. **A HALLWAY BETWEEN ROOMS.** It takes just a few steps to move through the area connecting the foyer to the living room in this home in Cambridge, Massachusetts. We invested in architectural upgrades, like reclaimed stone floors and hand-cut, antique mirrored tiles for the walls, and kept the furnishings to a minimum. At night, the homeowners dim the French, 1940s sconces and this space glows.

3

1

2

IMPACTFUL OBJECTS

Less is more in these in-between moments—and by that, I mean *fewer* pieces with *more* interesting detail. A few categories to consider:

1. An interesting arrangement at the end of a hall.
2. A vintage chair in front of a window.
3. Oversized pottery on the floor.

3

PLEASE PAUSE FOR

STAIRCASES

If you've ever toured a neighborhood of new homes, you may have noticed that most of the staircases are identical—whether you were in a Cape Cod, an American farmhouse, or a Tudor. It is a decision that saved the builder money, but has very little stylistic integrity.

Historically, a staircase was a moment of atmosphere, an architectural feature that represented the quality of the rest of the home. I smile when I think about Morris Lapidus, an architect who worked in the 1960s. He built a grand, sweeping staircase in the lobby of an NYC apartment building that led to nowhere. It just stopped at the ceiling. I remember as a young designer being shocked by this: What was the purpose? It turns out, Lapidus wanted people who lived in the building to have a beautiful place to take a photo on their way out when dressed for dinner.

That story reminds me why staircases are so important. If an architect in the '60s designed a staircase to nowhere, and the staircases that I work on lead to everywhere, it feels especially important to get the details right.

A plaster banister with a gentle bend feels classically modern in this Palm Springs, California, home.

There are no sharp corners or unnecessary details on this multilevel staircase, a work of structural genius by architects Jennifer Lyford and Steve Hart for our project in Cambridge, Massachusetts. The white oak handrails have a graceful bend that required segmenting the railing into more than six sections before assembling it on site.

ANATOMY OF A STAIRCASE

Whether you're designing a staircase from scratch or looking to update something existing, consider the following:

- **RAILINGS:** Researching homes built in the same era and language as yours can help you choose a style (classic or modern) and materials (iron, oak, plaster, glass, etc.) that will work with your existing architecture. Do you need railings that are segmented, or is it possible to create a continuous flow?
- **RUNNERS:** If you have young children or pets, invest in carpeting for your stairs. I like wool runners for these high-traffic zones; they wear well.
- **SHAPE:** Changing the shape of an existing staircase is an astronomical investment that I don't recommend unless it is part of a large renovation. If you are starting a project from scratch, consider a curved or angled option, which are more fluid and gracious.

& ANOTHER THING . . .

If you inherited a staircase that you don't love, you can make cosmetic changes: upgrade the newel post, handrails, or balustrades. Consult an architect or a structural engineer who understands local building codes. Changing one component could mean you have to bring the whole staircase up to code, so do your homework before jumping in.

BATHROOMS

Designing a bathroom is about two things for me: finding creative places to put everything, and making the room feel luxurious. I always start with the what-goes-where of it all, and then also think about the following:

- Where is the natural light coming from? If it's an option, I will always place the vanity as close to a window as possible.
- What other light do you need? Recessed lighting is a must, but balance them with interesting sconces and a great ceiling fixture.
- Is it possible to add architecture in a thoughtful way? An arched shower entry or decorative moulding bring warmth and a sense of history to a space that can feel too spare.
- Is there room to include furniture? It is unexpected in these spaces. (Turn to page 268 for some ideas.)

An interesting mix of materials is important, even here. This tub is carved from a single piece of marble. It sits on an aged wood floor and is framed by dark marble baseboards and trim. The natural rug brings texture, while the French, 1950s side table—a combination of glass, iron, and brass—elevates the space.

WHATEVER YOU DO, PLEASE DON'T . . .

- **BE AFRAID OF WOOD FLOORS.** They are softer to walk on than stone or tile, and, as long as you use a rug near your shower, surprisingly durable.
- **CLAD YOUR BATHROOM ENTIRELY IN MARBLE,** unless that is your dream. I like more layers—stone with woods, terracotta, and metals, like iron and bronze.
- **FOLLOW TRENDS.** The main components of this room are a big investment, so stick with classic materials that will age well.

While re-designing a small bathroom in Manhattan, our clients requested two sinks, but the space available would typically allow for only one. (The standard minimum vanity length for two sinks is 60 inches.) We used slightly smaller sinks to accommodate the request and made up for the lack of counter space by selecting larger medicine cabinets.

Aesop.

LET'S TALK ABOUT VANITIES

A typical vanity has four main components: lighting, a mirror, cabinetry, and a sink/faucet combination. Let your style and maximizing function determine the material choices you make. Do you need more storage or more counter space? Is this where you put on makeup in the morning; if so, do you need an added layer of lighting? Don't let function be the only priority. Include at least one unexpected detail to make the space feel fresh. Here are a few ideas to consider.

1. **FLUTED WOOD DRAWERS** add architectural detail.
2. **VANITY LIGHTS ON THE SIDE WALLS** diffuse natural light coming from the window behind.
3. **AN ORNAMENTAL BACKSPLASH**, like the shaped one here, turns a moment of practicality into a moment of beauty.
4. **WOVEN METAL** upgrades a cabinet door with the added benefit of airflow.

1
2
3
4

LET'S TALK ABOUT SHOWER WALLS

Bardiglio Blue Venato marble.

	MARBLE
WHY TO LOVE IT	• Natural stone is luxurious. • In a contained area you can experiment with busier veining without it becoming overwhelming. • Minimal grout lines prevent mildew.
WHY TO SKIP IT	• The cost of full slabs and specialized installation make using this material an expensive endeavor. • Over time, patination and staining will occur, which happens with all marble and natural stone. • There are more creative—less expensive—ways to use marble. (See page 266.)

Zellige tiles in a basketweave pattern.

SureCrete decorative concrete.

TILE	WATERPROOF CEMENT COATING
• The material selection is extensive: porcelain, ceramic, clay, natural stone. • You can find almost any color, pattern, or finish. • In handmade options, there is a beautiful imperfection that can't be replicated.	• You can apply it directly on top of old tile. • No grout means you won't spend your weekend scrubbing the shower. • You can color match it to the exact shade of the walls.
• Working with a professional installer is a costly but necessary investment. • There is no easy fix for a broken tile; if one cracks, it might require retiling a whole section of the shower. • Grout lines are a commitment to upkeep.	• The texture is similar to concrete. • It can crack over time and will require some maintenance/touch-ups. • A lot of contractors are nervous to use it. They would rather work with actual concrete, which lasts longer.

LET'S TALK ABOUT SHOWER ENCLOSURES

FRAMED GLASS DOORS. I gravitate to brass frames that feel slightly industrial.

SHOWER CURTAINS. They allow you to change the look and style of your bathroom quickly and easily.

METAL ENCLOSURES. The style reminds me of an English greenhouse and feels just as charming in a bathroom.

FRAMELESS GLASS. Minimal and clean; you get more credit for your tile selection.

EVERY BATHROOM NEEDS A LUXURIOUS MOMENT . . .

ABOVE: Reach for elevated finishes in a vanity: Antique glass panels, a French, 1970s brass mirror, and a vintage leopard print stool are timeless and glamorous.

OPPOSITE: I designed this room with a freestanding tub over twenty years ago for an actress and busy mom, whose main wish was for a place to disconnect.

LET'S TALK ABOUT JIB DOORS

Jib doors blend seamlessly into the walls and are especially practical for disguising storage in a bathroom. Shallow shelves can fit between the studs of your walls. In our NYC bathroom, Jeremiah and I have them in two places: next to our vanity (instead of medicine cabinets) and in the water closet. If you're renovating, and your walls are already open, including a jib door to hide a cabinet is a smart addition.

ORGANIZING THE BATHROOM WITH JULIA PINSKY

Founder of the Pinsky Project, a home organizing company on the West Coast, Julia Pinsky's work is meticulous and well-documented; a scroll through her Instagram of pantries, perfectly divided drawers, and color-coded closets is a dream. Here's how she suggests tackling a bathroom.

- **SEPARATE YOUR ITEMS INTO CATEGORIES:** hair, body, face, dental, medicine, first aid, and so on. Ideally, each category has its own drawer. If that is not an option, group categories but use drawer dividers to keep the order.
- **MINIMIZE COUNTERTOP CLUTTER.** Hand soap and lotion, toothbrushes, and possibly a pretty tray of perfumes should be the only things on your counter.
- **KEEP AN EDITED SHOWER SHELF.** Only the products you use daily should live there. Find another place to store anything that is not a part of your regular routine.
- **UTILIZE THE VERTICAL SPACE UNDER YOUR SINK.** Freestanding drawer units are useful here. Invest in a lazy Susan for hair tools.

The vanities in our former LA bathroom included affordable nickel medicine cabinets. We framed them in a Venetian-inspired shaped marble (leftover from our shower renovation) and added a small shelf. A reminder that practical can be elegant, too.

STRATEGIC WAYS TO USE MARBLE

I consider a design to be successful when the time and money spent to create a detail are equal to its impact. I have always thought a bathroom clad entirely in marble—which is not a small investment—isn't the most interesting option.

I like to use stone to elevate architectural details like baseboards or door surrounds, or to create a single important feature in the room. This is a good way to use a luxurious material and stay within your budget. Buy fewer slabs but be more deliberate with where you use them. Here are few ideas to consider.

1. Two book-matched slabs create a focal point for the vanity wall; the rest of the room is simple.

2. Traditional moulding is elevated in marble, replacing wood baseboards and framing the shower.

3. A modern custom vanity with two hidden drawers in Calacatta Paonazzo.

4. A luxurious tub surround in Calacatta Viola; tile, not marble slabs, were used on the floor.

1

2

3

4

ADDING FURNITURE IN THE BATHROOM

In a room that is typically bright and clean, there is something gracious about incorporating furniture: a small side table, a chair, a chest of drawers. It is an opportunity to introduce warmer materials—wood, leather, or even velvet—to balance the tile, stone, and metal. Something old that doesn't feel so polished works well.

A nineteenth-century center table creates a beautiful moment.

A vintage bench adds warmth and character next to the bath.

An armoire, instead of built-in cabinetry, brings personality and history to the mix.

A comfortable chair in original leather from the 1930s is an unexpected luxury.

THE MOMENTS
THAT MAKE THE ROOM

TRY A WARM SHADE ON THE WALLS. When Jeremiah and I moved back into our NYC apartment, we used hand-applied decorative plaster on the walls of our bathroom, which were originally white. The shade and texture made the fixtures and fittings feel warmer, while the vintage figural painting above the tub (a piece by Thomas Leyland we bought at auction) brings charm and character.

CONSIDER REUPHOLSTERING A CHAIR OR STOOL IN A TOWEL, something I have done often. Terrycloth is durable and so comfortable to sit on when you're half dressed and getting ready for your day.

DECORATIVE CONTAINERS ARE FUN TO FIND: handsome cups, little baskets, small pottery. I always keep an eye out for thoughtful storage solutions that look good on display.

ALWAYS MOUNT A HOOK BY THE SHOWER. My mother, on one of her first trips to visit us in New York City, said she was not staying unless I put something on the wall to hang her towel from.

MY BEST ADVICE ON WHERE TO SPEND & WHERE TO SAVE

SPEND ON . . .

- Stone
- Bathroom fixtures
- Lighting
- Hiring skilled tradespeople (tile installers, plumbers, etc.)

SAVE ON . . .

- Medicine cabinets
- Vintage accessories for your vanity
- Towels
- Bath rugs
- Hardware for your cabinets (there are great options on Etsy)

POWDER ROOMS

To understand someone's personal style, visit their powder room. In this space, even the most hardwired traditionalist can be inspired to take a few risks. Use a bold wallpaper. Find a salvaged stone sink. This is one of the few places where you can push your creative vision. When guests visit the powder room in our home, they are greeted by a sculptural light fixture shaped like a spider from the 1950s climbing antique mirrored walls (see page 13).

Lean into texture and definition. For clients in Palm Springs, California, we chose lighting (French lanterns from the 1960s by Arlus Lighting) and heavily textured plaster walls that bring modern details to the small space.

WHATEVER YOU DO, PLEASE DON'T . . .

- **BE NERVOUS ABOUT TAKING A COMPLETE DEPARTURE AESTHETICALLY IN THIS SPACE.** It can have its own language.
- **FORGET THIS ROOM IS FOR GUESTS.** Pay attention to the details: Have nice containers for your hand soap and lotion, a place for fresh flowers, and room spray.
- **HANG A PLAIN MIRROR.** There are great vintage options, which don't have to be expensive, that can introduce an interesting shape or new material.

SMALL SPACE, BIG IMPACT

I have always loved designing powder rooms. It's the easiest place for me to convince clients to do something they would never do anywhere else, especially on the walls. Here are a few ideas to help get you in the right mindset to step out of your comfort zone.

EXAGGERATED TEXTURE. Grasscloth or paper-backed fabrics add warmth to any room.

NOT YOUR AVERAGE STRIPE. Osmunda wallpaper by Soane Britain and other vertical patterns are great in tight spaces because they create an illusion of height.

OVER-THE-TOP PATTERN. Hermès's Dune wallpaper has a subtle texture that makes it look hand-painted.

ARCHITECTURAL UPGRADES. Simple and cost effective, this moulding treatment is something you can do yourself using pre-cut and finished trim from a hardware store and a nail gun.

YOUR WALLS AS A CANVAS

This powder room is part of a project I worked on for over three years in Seattle. My firm was almost through the design, and we still had not landed on a direction for the powder room, when I saw a mural behind the counter of a store in Minneapolis. The artist turned out to be a local painter named Sarah Burns. We flew her to Seattle to hand-paint the walls of this bathroom. If you follow any artists in your area, think about ways to collaborate. Nothing makes design feel more special than the story behind how it came to life.

LET'S TALK ABOUT VANITIES (AGAIN)

In a primary bathroom, function and storage have to be a priority. In powder rooms you can be a bit more liberal, choose things based on what makes a statement on style alone. What will surprise and delight people when they walk in? What will they least expect to see? Don't shy away from the dramatic choice.

1. **CONSIDER A NON-TRADITIONAL SINK.** This stone sink began its life as a baptismal font (or stoup) in a church somewhere in nineteenth-century Europe and brings history and patination to the space.
2. **A GALLERY LIGHT FEELS UNEXPECTED,** and is especially lovely when the finish ties together the other components in the room.
3. **USE FABRIC TRIM TO FRAME THE WALLS.** Decorative borders—like the line of brown cotton tape along the ceiling of this bathroom—can be glued around windows or doorways, and make a space feel polished.

1

RIGHT: Monogrammed hand towels are a thoughtful touch. Jeremiah and I have a collection of linen towels embroidered with *BB* in our powder room. I have always loved the tradition behind monograms: in the late nineteenth century, families would pass down intricate bits of cloth from one generation to the next. A small investment—of time, not money—that became an heirloom.

OPPOSITE: The scale of the wallpaper (a print by Pierre Frey) is exaggerated and bold, but the fixtures—a custom Nero Marquina scalloped sink, a 1960s French bamboo mirror, even the towel ring—are petite. The contrast opens up the room, making it appear much bigger than 65 square feet.

7

ROOMS TO GROW

Kids' Bedrooms | Kids' Bathrooms
Spaces for Homework

KIDS' BEDROOMS

When designing spaces for the smaller members of the family my best advice is to invest in pieces that will grow with them. Including vintage furniture and objects that come with built-in patina, pieces that could move with them to their first apartment one day, is how you create a space that is *meaningful*. Instead of buying a new changing table from a website, something Oskar would have outgrown in a few months, Jeremiah and I found an antique English chest of drawers for him, attached a changing pad on top for the months we needed it, and stored all his diapers and creams in a drawer. Well-made furniture not only stands the test of time, it will stand the test of living with toddlers, preteens, and teenagers. Here are a few other ideas to try:

- Choose artwork that is kid-friendly without being so cute they outgrow it.
- Whimsy is a touchpoint I use a lot, especially in terms of styling. There is a way to achieve this that has longevity. (Turn to page 290.)
- My avoidance of furniture assembled with an Allen wrench has two notable exceptions: a crib and a bassinet, neither of which you need forever.

RIGHT: When we moved back into our NYC home, Oskar wanted his room to have the same wallpaper (Sur le Nil by Pierre Frey) that he had in our townhouse. He really liked all the animals. Providing a visual through line, a connection between what he knew and what *was* new, was like wrapping the room in a familiar blanket. It instantly put him at ease.

PREVIOUS PAGE: Be open to layering patterns. Florals, vines, and geometrics all sharing the same space feels fun and energetic.

WHATEVER YOU DO, PLEASE DON'T . . .

- **AVOID COLOR IN THIS SPACE**. Even if you're a fan of neutrals, these rooms thrive with pronounced hues and playful patterns.
- **OVERLOOK PIECES THAT MAXIMIZE STORAGE.** The number of tiny things children have and need a home for is shocking.
- **BUY AN EXPENSIVE RUG**. I have yet to find one that can hold up long-term to the daily wear and tear and spills. Find something on sale and know that you'll likely have to replace it often.

DON'T BE AFRAID TO USE ANTIQUES

Old things do not *have* to be precious. They can be sturdy and practical—and harder to destroy than you may think. I tell this to clients all the time, when they get nervous about what their child will do to the furniture in their bedroom. Oskar went through a phase where he taped his LEGO men to everything in our home: the walls, the furniture, the floor. But you know what, it all survived.

This isn't the place for a family heirloom or an important piece of expensive furniture. But it is the right moment for an old armoire you found at a flea market or an antique Swedish desk you spotted at an estate sale. I think trusting your child with things, explaining the history behind them, teaches them to appreciate and care for their belongings.

---

1. **PETITE CHESTS OF DRAWERS** are something I am always bringing into kids' rooms, where you can't have too many places to store things. Nineteenth-century Swedish furniture works particularly well because it is smaller in scale.
2. **AN ANTIQUE CABINET** is a handsome (and solid) storage solution. My design partner, Lauren, keeps her son, Reid's, books and other treasures inside a nineteenth-century French armoire.
3. **SOMETHING HAND-PAINTED** feels special. This Danish laundry cabinet from the 1960s looks like a dresser, but there is actually a door that swings open to reveal five shelves inside.
4. **AN OVERSIZED VINTAGE ARMCHAIR** in a (virtually) indestructible fabric is a cozy spot for bedtime stories.

1

2

3

Rr
4

When people see this image of Poppy's bedroom, they ask where the toys are. The vintage folding screen behind her headboard is hiding a Barbie village. The shelves inside the nineteenth-century French armoire hold bins of doll accessories and art supplies. All the small things she needs are inside beautiful furniture so that you don't see the chaos the moment you walk through the door.

ORGANIZING A KIDS' BEDROOM WITH

JULIA PINSKY

THREE STEPS TO GETTING STARTED

STEP 1: DECLUTTER. Go through everything. Recycle or rehouse the following: clothes your kids have outgrown, toys they no longer play with, books they are too old for, outdated art projects. Kids will keep every single thing forever; be creative in how you convince them to part with their belongings.

STEP 2: CATEGORIZE. Start with the big categories, like board games, books, art supplies, and toys, and then get more specific. Art supplies could have a section for markers, crayons, paints, brushes, paper, and so forth. Then you can further divide things by color.

STEP 3: STORE. Every item you plan to keep should have a home. Develop a storage system that feels intuitive. The goal is to make it so easy that your kids can put everything away with little help from you.

OTHER CONSIDERATIONS

CONTAIN THE CHAOS OF TINY TREASURES. Put smaller items in labeled pouches that zip.

BUY STORAGE PRODUCTS FROM ONE SYSTEM. This ensures everything stacks neatly.

LABELED, CLEAR CONTAINERS MAKE LIFE EASIER. Your kids can see what's inside, so they don't have to open every box looking for their Transformers.

ORGANIZE BOOKS BY COLOR, THEN SIZE. When storing them on a long shelf, group books in small sections and add bookends between, which keeps the whole row from toppling over when your child goes to pull one book out.

KEEP ART SUPPLIES IN ONE PLACE. Divided bins and lazy Susans, or a tiered art cart on wheels all work well.

INTRODUCE AN ART BIN (OR DRAWER), a place to store art once its time on display is over. When the container is full, do an edit. Move the pieces you want to keep into long-term storage or have them digitized.

UNDER-THE-BED STORAGE IS A SPACE SAVER. You can find bins on wheels for off-season clothing and bedding.

CONSIDER REACHABILITY. Keep what they use most often lower to the floor.

DECLUTTER REGULARLY. Do a thorough sweep every four months if you can. Kids change quickly, and their stuff piles up fast.

STYLING GUIDE

KIDS' ROOMS

Picture the bedroom you grew up in. There is something about the way this space holds the memories of a younger-you that leaves a lasting and meaningful impression. Our childhood bedrooms are honest versions of who we are, an expression of our world through the twists and turns of being a kid, then a teenager.

When I am styling a kid's room, it is a careful balance. They should be beautiful and ignite the imagination with places for them to display their treasures: Rocks collected on the beach stacked on a windowsill, LEGO sets on a shelf. These expressions of love and play are the most important details.

A friend once told me that for her young boys, she used sheets printed with their favorite characters but kept the top of the beds sophisticated. The kids got their Mickey Mouse moment, but the bed didn't read like a toy store. I've always thought it was a great analogy for how to approach this space: creating a beautiful, high-functioning framework for them to consistently reimagine into their own world.

---

1. **GO AHEAD AND FRAME THEIR HEROES.** My client's fifteen-year-old son is a big basketball fan. We framed a poster of Michael Jordan's Nike ad, making it feel more grown-up—something he could hang in his office one day.
2. **LET THEM DISPLAY WHAT THEY LOVE.** The evolution of their choices, from school art projects to posters of their favorite musicians, is a beautiful way to witness their creativity.
3. **REMIND THEM YOU WERE ONCE THEIR AGE, TOO.** The leather pig in the corner of Oskar's room is from Liberty in London and makes me smile. I had a rhinoceros in my room when I was young, which now also lives in his bedroom.

ORIGIN STORIES

This upholstered bed is one of my favorite reminders to try to use what you already own. It was Poppy's first "big girl" bed (see page 292). We reupholstered it three times before moving it to Oskar's room and covering it in an army green military canvas sturdy enough to withstand his daily acrobatics.

Poppy and Oskar's art collections began organically and with deep meaning attached to each piece. The paintings in the photo above were a gift from James and Alexandra Brown. The small painting of the bird above the bed (right) is from our friend Michael Hainey. Support the artists in your area to find things that will be with your kids for a long time.

Poppy

THE PETITE (AND PERFECT) BEDROOM

If you've lived in the tight confines of a major city, then you know any nook or closet can be turned into a bedroom or a nursery. There is something both charming and very freeing about designing within spacial limitations. It simplifies the decision-making process to two main steps: Do I like this piece of furniture? Will it fit in the room?

When Oskar was born, we annexed part of Poppy's room to make a small bedroom for him at our house in Montauk, New York. It's six-feet wide, and fits a twin-sized bed and a chest of drawers. Despite its size, its design ticks all the important boxes: a vintage alabaster lamp on an antique stool used as a bedside table; a simple headboard with Jeremiah's embroidered blanket folded over it; a South American macramé swordfish we found at a craft show in NYC. Something old. Something interesting. Something with a story to tell.

LEFT: The smaller the room, the more natural light it needs. Oskar's bedroom in Montauk has a wall-sized window overlooking the backyard that makes its 175 square feet seem bigger.

OPPOSITE: Creating the illusion of space where there isn't much: In this 120 square-foot guest room in Manhattan, we used the same cotton ticking-stripe fabric on everything; the continuity makes the walls appear to recede.

ANOTHER THING . . .

Almost any fabric can be a wallcovering if you have it paper backed. A lot of the big fabric houses (Schumacher, for example) will do this for you, but you can also search online to find someone local.

Sharing a bedroom with a sibling, as I did with my brother, is a rite of passage. If you have the space, built-in bunk beds—whether one set or two—give each child their own area. This configuration in Chicago includes a full-size bed below and a twin up top.

DESIGNING A KIDS' BATHROOM

Embracing color and pattern and being more playful with the objects you choose is as important in a kid's bathroom as it is in their bedroom. Make decisions that will age well. As fun as it is to involve your child in the process, try not to cave to their every whim. Committing to a *Cars*-themed bathroom because your three year-old loves that movie is essentially committing to another decorating project in a year.

Lean into the classics when selecting tile, flooring, fixtures, or anything that requires hiring someone to install it. You can be more whimsical with everything else. Buy patterned towels, or use a saturated paint color or a bright shower curtain.

RIGHT: Enamel tubs can be painted, which was common in Victorian homes, where claw-foot baths were the norm. It's a way to add color in an unexpected place.

OPPOSITE: Lighting is another opportunity to introduce something adventurous. The pop of red from Jean Royère's "Bouquet" sconce is energetic against the soft green walls.

My firm designed this multipurpose space for a family with three young boys. The custom bookcases, a combination of open and closed storage, allow them to display personal objects and hide everything else.

WORKSPACES FOR KIDS

A designated place to work is an important moment to carve out for kids. We always include one in homes we design for families, no matter how small of an area we are able to assign to the task. A desk or table, an appropriately sized chair, a lamp, and an organizational system are essential. It also has to be a place they *want* to spend time, which is why I reach for shapes that have some whimsy: a chair with a scalloped back, a lamp that looks like it could be a mushroom—things that are durable *and* playful.

1. **STARING AT A PLAIN WALL GETS OLD.** Consider adding wallpaper, or hanging a bulletin board or grouping of artwork.
2. **INCLUDE A MIX OF INFLUENCES.** A French-style painted desk paired with a fun wicker chair is classic and energetic.
3. **POSITION THE DESK FACING A WINDOW,** if you can. It's a happier way to work.

1

THE MOMENTS
THAT MAKE THE ROOM

A LITTLE WHIMSY GOES A LONG WAY.
A stuffed monkey sitting on a framed photograph (see page 298). Favorite dolls that live on top of an antique lantern. Serious furniture that feels playful because it's upholstered in a pretty pattern with stuffed animals perched on the seat. Have some fun with how you display the things they love.

REPURPOSE FURNITURE YOU ALREADY OWN. In Oskar's nursery, we used a woven wicker and iron bar cart from the 1950s as a side table next to his crib. It held a small vintage lamp and his favorite bedtime storybooks. The same piece now lives in my New York City office, and we use it to serve drinks to clients.

TONE DOWN THE COLOR CHOICES. As much as your children may want bright red or royal blue walls, try to take it down a few shades. It will look better for longer.

THEIR NAME IN LIGHTS. When we were designing Oskar's room, we found a place on Etsy to customize his name in neon (see page 291). We didn't expect it to be such a hit. Poppy has her own, and we had another made for our playroom that says: "My heart loves your heart." These lights are now a special part of our family's story.

MY BEST ADVICE ON WHERE TO SPEND & WHERE TO SAVE

SPEND ON . . .

- A chest of drawers that can grow with them
- A beautiful lamp
- Wallpaper
- Framing your artwork
- Custom cabinetry
- A desk

SAVE ON . . .

- A rug
- The crib/bassinet (as long as its well-made)
- Decorative pillows
- Bedding
- Cute decorations
- Baskets for toys

8

ROOMS TO WORK

Home Offices | Workspaces

HOME OFFICES

When our professional lives went digital five years ago and our in-person meetings were replaced by Zooms, finding a comfortable place to be productive at home became essential—whether that meant working from a bedroom, a corner of the kitchen, or the end of a table. We started to think about how to make our home offices inspiring destinations *and* to worry about what people saw in the background during meetings. What do the book titles on the shelf say about us as people? Is this lighting flattering? The design lens shifted from "what do I like?" to "what will people think?," which is not the ideal mindset to create a space that feels personal.

My advice is to worry less about what people see on Zoom and more about what *you* look at all day. Style the bookcase, hang things you love, create a space that feels in sync with who you are and what you do. Here are some ways to accomplish that:

- Start with the essentials: a great surface to work on and a comfortable chair to sit in.
- Consider your sightlines when creating a floorplan. (See page 310.)
- Position your desk to face a window, if possible.
- Create storage that is both functional and beautiful.

RIGHT: I love to include things in a home office that inspire curiosity and conversation. The photograph on the wall (*L'homme qui fume*, 1971) is by photographer Sanlé Sory, who documented the cultural shift of his country as it transitioned from French Upper Volta to Burkina Faso in 1984.

PREVIOUS PAGE: When I am at my office in NYC, I sit at a repurposed dining table. They typically have a larger surface, are easier to find, and have more character than a desk.

WHATEVER YOU DO, PLEASE DON'T . . .

- **DECORATE TO THE POINT OF DISTRACTION**. Subtlety is the goal.
- **MAKE EVERYTHING IN THE ROOM UTILITARIAN**. A handsome cup for pens or a silver bowl for paperclips are small things that elevate your day.
- **LET THE SPACE FUNCTION AS A CATCHALL**. This is not the place for overflow from the rest of your house.

LET'S TALK ABOUT SIGHT LINES

The first thing to ask yourself about this space should be: What will make you happy to look at all day? Let your answer guide the furniture placement. Try sitting in a few different spots until you find what feels right, then create a floorplan around that.

The location of the desk will define the flow of the room. Centering it feels formal and classic. For something more unexpected, try it on an angle: A desk slightly askew by a window, or on the diagonal in a corner. These rooms show some of my favorite desk and chair combinations, and ideas for their placement.

1. **A NINETEENTH-CENTURY, EMPIRE-STYLE DESK + A LOW-PROFILE OFFICE CHAIR.** We were able to position the arrangement in a corner by the window, instead of in the middle of the room, because the antique desk is small.

2. **A VINTAGE CONSOLE + A HIGH-BACK CHAIR ON CASTORS.** This Seattle office overlooks the home's formal living room with an unobstructed view of the antique fireplace.

3. **A 1970S GLASS-TOP DINING TABLE + A VINTAGE LEATHER SWIVEL CHAIR.** This table sits in the corner of a living room in Milan. It is used as a desk most days, but seats overflow guests for dinner parties.

4. **A WRITING DESK + A LEATHER ARMCHAIR.** We arranged this small workspace in front of the window in a sunny enclave off the main bedroom.

1

2

3

4

What was a rarely used library became a beautifully appointed place to work at home.

KLEE
PIERO PORTALUPPI
Vincent Van Duysen
Works 2009 – 2018

STYLING GUIDE

THE HOME OFFICE

You spend more hours looking at the objects on your desk than any other accessories in your home. How you curate this space matters. Styling and organizing are equally important. Bring in objects that are handsome and functional: a silver bowl for paperclips, a leather tray for mail, a blown-glass tumbler for pens.

MAKE IT FEEL LIKE HOME. My desktop holds things I really love that remind me of home. I keep my binder clips in an antique silver bowl and family photos in vintage leather frames are grouped in a corner.

ORIGIN STORIES

The Art Deco silver box on my desk, which holds pens, was a gift from my management team. I used to joke that all the businesses I am involved in feel like a banana cart sometimes. So the inscription inside says, "Here's to our banana cart." Thoughtful and funny, I will have it forever.

CONSIDER ADDING SLANTED SHELVES TO YOUR CABINETRY. Favorite book covers become art when displayed this way.

STYLING TO INSPIRE. This carved figure represents classic Roman culture, which reminds me to always look for timeless details when designing. The South American necklace reminds me to remain whimsical. This vignette is like a Post-it note, reconfirming my design foundations in a glance.

FINDING A PLACE TO WORK

Most of us, me included, don't have the luxury of a dedicated home office. We have to be more creative, finding space in hallways and corners of rooms to work from. Here are some of my favorite places to squeeze in a workspace.

1

1. The family room office.
2. The bedroom office.
3. The kitchen office.
4. The closet office.
5. The hallway office.

2

3

4

5

ABOVE: For a busy entrepreneur who often works from home an adjacent wet bar was worth investing in. It allows him to fully detach from the rest of the house during work hours. A simpler option would be to set up a coffee station or add a stocked (and handsomely styled) bar cart.

RIGHT: The couple who bought this nineteenth-century home wanted to push its classic, preppy roots to feel more international and cosmopolitan—more like them. In the office, we used white oak for all the trim, and leather panels on the wall. Textured wallpaper or paper-backed fabrics would bring a similar richness.

A SOFT PLACE TO LAND

Don't let your desk chair be the only place to sit in this space. Give yourself a less formal option: a small sofa where you can take a call, a pair of club chairs, even two upholstered stools at a small round table. You will enjoy the versatility.

1

DO YOU HAVE ROOM FOR...

1. **AN EDITED SEATING ARRANGEMENT?** This grouping allows you to have a casual meeting with more than three people—and doubles as a secondary space to entertain.

2. **AN UPHOLSTERED ARMCHAIR?** So you don't have to have every conversation sitting behind a desk.

3. **A SIDE CHAIR?** Any corner is an opportunity to add a handsome and practical grouping.

LET'S TALK ABOUT STORAGE

Home offices need a well-planned organizational system to function. Shelving is a necessity, whether you bring in freestanding bookshelves or build something custom. If you can, I recommend the latter, even if it is a "plan now, install later" investment. Having everything exactly where you need it to be, and having something that increases the value of your home, is always a good decision. Here are a few more ideas to help keep you organized:

- **USE TRAYS TO STORE THINGS**, which can work better than drawers. In my office, we built a tower of shelves, where we stack project trays that hold material samples.
- **HIDE ELECTRICAL EQUIPMENT.** Installing pull-out shelves in your cabinetry will make tasks like changing an ink cartridge easier.
- **BE SPECIFIC ABOUT WHAT YOU NEED.** The more granular you are with the details, the more efficient you can be with planning your space.

RIGHT: My firm upgraded the cabinetry in this office with bronze metal grilles, typically used to cover radiators. They add detail and texture, and also allow circulation so equipment doesn't overheat.

OPPOSITE: We flanked the sofa in this Manhattan office with a set of built-in cabinets. When closed, the mouldings mask the openings, so the high-gloss walls have a continuous flow.

THE MOMENTS

THAT MAKE THE ROOM

LOCATION. LOCATION. LOCATION. If you have the luxury of choosing where to have a home office, pick an area that feels like a destination: a space at the end of a hallway, a small room on the quiet side of the house, a corner of a guest room that's infrequently used. Find somewhere that gives you a sense of separation from your daily life.

LOOK FOR PLACES TO PERSONALIZE. It can be meaningful no matter how small. For our client in Seattle, we monogrammed the cabinet knobs with their initials—a thoughtful touch that takes little effort to execute.

ONE STRONG, GRAPHIC ELEMENT IS ALL YOU NEED. Bold artwork or printed pillows work well without feeling chaotic. The geometric print on this rug, for instance, stands out because the room is mainly solids.

AN INTERESTING DESK LAMP IS A GOOD START. I like to include a lot of lighting sources for versatility: floor lamps, wall-mounted sconces, gallery lights on cabinetry, and task lighting built into the shelving system.

MY BEST ADVICE ON WHERE TO SPEND & WHERE TO SAVE

SPEND ON . . .

- Custom cabinetry
- Furniture for storage
- A beautiful desk
- A desk lamp
- An exceedingly comfortable desk chair

SAVE ON . . .

- Rugs
- Small storage solutions (drawer dividers, baskets, etc.)
- Books (search your local used bookstores)
- Window treatments (try to work with a standard, store-bought option, rather than custom)

9

ROOMS FOR THINGS

Closets | Laundry Rooms
Mudrooms | Pantries

CLOSETS

I like when a closet feels like walking into a store, a place where you can be surrounded by the beautiful things you have collected over a lifetime. It is a luxury that brings joy to your day. Some may argue that it is a lot of effort spent on a space to store things, but here is why I think it is effort well spent: whether you have a closet you *walk* into or a wall of wardrobes in your bedroom you *reach* into, how you organize your clothes and accessories makes it easier for you to express your personal style. Here are a few things you can prioritize to make this space a better place to be:

- A closet should have its own organizational language. (Turn to page 342 for more on this.)
- Create a system and invest in products that make it easy to maintain.
- If you have the space, add at least one piece of decorative furniture.
- A soft rug or carpeting goes a long way in creating atmosphere.

RIGHT: For a fashion designer in Montecito, California—a project created in collaboration with Jeremiah Brent Design—we included custom-cut mirrored wardrobe doors, which bounce the natural light into the darkest corners of the room.

PREVIOUS PAGE: To be great at organizing, you have to take stock of what you currently own, while factoring in what you *might* own someday. Leaving space to grow means the closet you've spent time and money planning will meet your needs for a lot longer.

WHATEVER YOU DO, PLEASE DON'T . . .

- **INVITE CHAOS IN**. It's not welcome in this space, which means taking the time to put things away.
- **SKIP THE FOLDING TUTORIALS ON SOCIAL MEDIA**. Natasha Swingler (@effectivespaces) and Lennia McCarter (@lenniamc) are two people who have taught me a lot.
- **DESIGN A ROOM THAT'S ALL FUNCTION, NO MOOD**. A strong point of view will tie everything together.

OPEN VS. CLOSED STORAGE

There are two main options when planning a custom dressing room: leave everything out where you can see it or put your belongings behind closed doors. When making the decision, the question you need to ask yourself is: How committed to staying organized am I? If you are the type of person who transfers dry cleaning when it comes home to velvet hangers before putting everything away, then out and open will work for you. If you are not *that* organized, then I would suggest storing your things behind wardrobe doors in your closet. It allows you to feel less overwhelmed if the clothes you washed and folded on Saturday don't make it into drawers or onto hangers until later in the week.

LEFT: Jeremiah and I divided this space in two: The front section has curved rods that hold favorite pieces—evening gowns with beautiful bags above—while the back area has multiple banks of closed storage (see page 328) for everything else.

RIGHT: Wardrobe doors are another way to introduce additional finishes in this space, like antique mirrored panels or gathered fabric behind glass (shown here).

THIS HANDSOME DRESSING ROOM IN MONTECITO, CALIFORNIA, was inspired by a 1960s private club in London. Jeremiah and I tried to capture the feeling by using a soft, saturated carpet with dark wood cabinetry and vintage Italian glass pendants.

MY FIRST "GROWN-UP" CLOSET IN CHICAGO; the millwork was original, but I removed the doors and painted the wood a deep, muted blue. For texture, I added grasscloth on the walls and a striped runner found in Mexico. The way this space suddenly felt like me with minimal effort is woven into the foundation of my approach to design—even so many years later.

CREATING A MOOD

I have friends who regularly hang out in each other's closets. These utilitarian spaces can also be relaxing destinations. There is something comfortable about a dressing room when you give it a personal point of view. You want to slow down and linger. Here are some of my favorite ways to create a welcoming atmosphere.

1. **HAVE SOMEWHERE BEAUTIFUL FOR YOUR EYE TO LAND.** An arrangement of personal objects, like framed photos, feel very meaningful—a quick nod to where you've been as you get yourself ready for where you're going.

2. **INCLUDE A COMFORTABLE PLACE TO SIT:** a single chair, a pair of benches, or a small sofa. It is a quiet spot to sit and take a call.

3. **PRIORITIZE LIGHTING.** There are two goals here: functional lighting for getting dressed and atmospheric lighting (a table lamp, gallery lights) to help set a mood. You want to have both.

2

3

IN FAVOR OF THE CLOSET VANITY

In 2014, The Metropolitan Museum of Art in NYC had an exhibition called *Metropolitan Vanities: The History of the Dressing Table*, which explored how this furniture came to "epitomize the modern concept of glamour and luxury" during the Art Deco period in both Europe and America. If you've watched classic Hollywood films from the 1920s and 1930s, they almost all include a scene where the heroine sits at an elegant vanity applying lipstick or putting on jewelry; the height of sophistication of that era.

Dressing tables fell out of fashion as bathrooms grew and became more modern, fitted with cabinets, mirrors, and built-in vanities. But I have always thought that having a quiet place to retreat *outside* of your bathroom to prepare for your day is glamorous in an accessible way, an opportunity to create a ritual around getting ready that could shift the energy of your morning.

ORIGIN STORIES

Finnish designer Olavi Hänninen's 1960s "King" Chair brings so much personality to this space; it is sculptural, raw, and striking in a polished setting.

1. **DON'T BE AFRAID OF HIGHLY DECORATIVE FINISHES**. This NYC closet, designed in the early 2000s in collaboration with architect Ahmad Sardar-Afkhami, is inspired by 1930s Art Deco grandeur with a vintage mirrored vanity, French plaster sconces, hand silver-leafed walls, and blown-glass knobs.

2. **USE MATERIALS WISELY.** We created a floating dressing table for a young mom in Chicago from marble remnants leftover from another project.

3. **CREATE A FOCAL POINT.** In this home, you pass through the dressing room to get to the bedroom. When you open the door, your eye goes to this very pretty moment and not a wall of shirts and shoes.

BUILDING A CUSTOM CLOSET

It takes a tremendous amount of preplanning to get the framework of a closet right. I have always found designing them to be rewarding. The hyper-organization aligns perfectly with my triple Virgo need for order . . . I am someone who watches folding videos for fun.

A closet can function and also be elegant. It starts with taking a detailed inventory of everything you own. When I designed Oprah's closet for her in the early 2000s, I measured each piece of jewelry to understand which drawer dividers I needed and how to configure them. Creating an organizational system in this way, one that makes the most of the space you have and is easy to maintain, will help you plan your closet's framework. Here are a few other things to consider:

- **BE THOUGHTFUL ABOUT SIGHT LINES.** If you look at one of my former closets on page 326, you'll notice that my T-shirts aren't the first thing you see; they're around the corner. I like to put suits or jackets at the forefront.
- **MAXIMIZE THE UTILITY OF YOUR FOUR EXISTING WALLS.** Can you alter the floorplan to create additional storage, include an island, wing walls (see photo at right), or shallow shelves to make your closet even more hardworking?
- **A GRID OF OPEN SHELVING IS INCREDIBLY PRACTICAL.** Rectangular compartments—14.5 inches wide by 6 inches high by 13 inches deep—allow you to stack and store multiple sweaters or jeans that will stay neatly folded.
- **FIND A CREATIVE WAY TO ADD DRAWERS**, whether you plan a built-in or leave an area open for a freestanding dresser, which will also give the space more style.
- **TAKE YOUR STORAGE TO THE CEILING.** A row of cabinets at the top of your closet is where you can store luggage and off-season clothing.
- **SLANTED SHOE SHELVES ARE MY PREFERENCE**, but they are typically built-in. If you are rotating shoes often, I recommend adjustable flat shelves that can be moved as needed.
- **INCLUDE A FULL-LENGTH MIRROR**—even if it's on the back of the door.

For our NYC closet, Jeremiah and I built wing walls with adjustable mirrors that pivot so you can see yourself from different angles. The small walls doubled our shoe storage, since we were able to have shelves on both sides, and created a division between my side of the closet and his.

WHEN YOU DON'T HAVE A WALK-IN CLOSET

If your closet is not its own designated room, there is a lot in this chapter that will still work for you. I have lived in and designed many homes where a wall of cabinets or even a large armoire in a hallway held all the clothes, shoes, and accessories. If this is your situation, then here is what you need to know:

- The sorting and organizing rules for clothes and accessories on page 342 still apply.
- Create a framework that combines custom and store-bought solutions to get the storage you need at a lower cost. Buying an inexpensive bookcase or chest of drawers and putting it *inside* your reach-in closet will give you more places to store things.
- Make every linear foot count by investing in products that maximize storage. Adjustable closet components allow you to slide in an extra shelf or double the hanging space.
- Look for ways to personalize store-bought closet systems by adding custom materials and nice hardware. At our home in Montauk, New York, we put grasscloth on the doors of an IKEA cabinet and found driftwood pulls on Etsy.

---

1. To create a custom wall of storage, you only need 2 feet of depth if you want to hang clothes inside.
2. I like to include at least one piece of furniture, something antique, like this Louis XVI–style dresser from the 1940s.
3. If you can't dedicate an entire wall to storage, adding banks of cabinetry flanking a fireplace or window is a great option.

ORGANIZING A CLOSET WITH

JULIA PINSKY

THREE STEPS TO GETTING STARTED

STEP 1: PULL OUT THE THINGS YOU LOVE. Instead of editing the pieces in your closet you *don't* wear first, start by gathering the clothes, shoes, and accessories you *do* wear, the items that make you happiest.

STEP 2: DECIDE WHAT ELSE TO KEEP. Don't hold on to something for sentimental reasons or because you spent a lot of money on it. Those items are just taking up space. If you're on the fence, try it on. Does it fit? Do you feel great in it? If the answer is "not anymore," then donate or resell it.

STEP 3: TAKE A DETAILED INVENTORY. How many pairs of pants do you own? How many shirts, sweaters, hats, and scarves? Measure the pieces that are not an average size: What is the length of your longest dress? How thick is your thickest coat? Then build a framework around those numbers. (On page 377 you will find a list of standard closet measurements that can help you convert your inventory list into shelf counts and hanging rail lengths.)

HELPFUL TIPS FOR ORGANIZING CLOTHES

ARRANGE CLOTHES BY CATEGORY, THEN BY COLOR. Within those groupings, I like to further break out pieces by dress code—casual versus formal.

DEVELOP A DRAWER HIERARCHY. Top drawers should contain underwear and socks. Middle drawers are always T-shirts, tank tops, and workout clothes. Bottom drawers store loungewear: pajamas, sweats, and bulkier items.

USE LABELED BINS FOR THINGS YOU DON'T WEAR REGULARLY, like ski clothes or anything that is holiday specific, and store them on a high shelf.

LEAVE ROOM FOR YOUR WARDROBE TO GROW. When planning closet storage, make sure to give yourself an extra shelf for new shoes, an extra foot on the hanging rail for new clothes, and some open space in your drawers.

MATCHING HANGERS ARE ESSENTIAL, preferably the nonslip kind.

INVEST IN DRAWER INSERTS. They allow you to *file* your folded tees vertically in a drawer, instead of *stacking* them, and make it easy to keep your folded pieces categorized.

HELPFUL TIPS FOR ORGANIZING SHOES

MEASURE YOUR FOOTWEAR. How tall are your tallest boots? How wide are your sneakers? These numbers help you determine how much shelf space you need.

ARRANGE YOUR SHOES BY STYLE, THEN BY COLOR. High heels together, sneakers together, flats together.

CUSTOM SHOE STORAGE WILL KEEP YOUR CLOSET NEATER. If every pair has a spot, it's easier to put them away.

HELPFUL TIPS FOR ORGANIZING ACCESSORIES

START WITH MEASUREMENTS (AGAIN). How wide is your biggest bag? What's the diameter of your sun hat? Create a detailed inventory, so you can design custom solutions for these tricky-to-organize pieces.

INCLUDE A JEWELRY DRAWER. Jewelry tray inserts or drawer dividers separate pieces by category and prevent necklaces from getting tangled.

STUFF YOUR HANDBAGS SO THEY KEEP THEIR SHAPE. Invest in silk "purse pillows" specifically made for this purpose, or roll up dust bags and tuck them inside.

I LOVE A HAT WALL FOR HANGING BIG HATS. Baseball caps look great lined up on a shelf, lightest to darkest.

HAVE A PLAN FOR BELTS AND TIES. A grid drawer insert works well, with each tie or belt rolled up in its own square.

EVERY CLOSET NEEDS A "JUNK" DRAWER, for things that don't have a home, like chargers and passports. Be sure to clear it out often.

THE MOMENTS
THAT MAKE THE ROOM

UNEXPECTED FURNITURE CHOICES WORK WELL HERE: an upholstered chaise lounge or a tête-à-tête sofa. I am drawn to these interesting shapes, but it can be tricky to find a place for them. In a closet, where you can do something a little bolder, they feel special.

GALLERY LIGHTS ARE ESPECIALLY GRACIOUS IN A DRESSING ROOM. In our NYC townhouse, we had to pass through the closet to get from our bedroom to the bathroom, so at night the gallery lights were on but dimmed low.

LEAVE ONE SHELF OPEN, FILL IT WITH HANDSOME OBJECTS. A simple arrangement of things that make you smile is a nice break in a room built around organization and function.

I LOVE AN OLD FRENCH CHANDELIER IN THIS SPACE, something romantic and sculptural, for the same reasons a vanity always feels glamorous. It is a nod to another era, when these rooms were more elegant.

MY BEST ADVICE ON WHERE TO SPEND & WHERE TO SAVE

SPEND ON . . .

- A custom or semi-custom cabinetry layout
- Spectacular central light fixtures
- Vintage or antique picture frames
- A great vintage bench

SAVE ON . . .

- Hangers
- Organizational items
- Shoe trees
- Lamp shades
- A runner

LAUNDRY ROOMS

When Jeremiah and I were renovating our last home, I think I discussed the laundry room—specifically the storage—with our architect more than any other room in the house. It is where I spend at least an hour of my day.

Laundry rooms are often the highest functioning spaces in a home. It is where the mountains of laundry land, where all the extra essentials are stored, and where the cleaning supplies are kept. Even a room with so many responsibilities can be beautiful to look at. I have always believed that good design can make completing the most mundane tasks more enjoyable, so here are a few tips to consider:

- Like a closet, this room needs an organizational language. (See page 352 for examples.)
- Decorative objects displayed on an open shelf or a windowsill bring warmth: framed photos, things found in nature, artwork (especially if your child is the artist).
- Try something bold, like a deeper color, stripes, or sculptural hardware.
- Before buying materials—flooring, countertops, hardware—shop your leftovers and the remnant section at your local stoneyard. I can't tell you how many laundry and mudroom floors I've covered with extra entry tiles.

If you have the space, I like to include an oversized cabinet in the laundry room to store large cleaning tools (mops, brooms, the vacuum cleaner) and laundry appliances.

WHATEVER YOU DO, PLEASE DON'T . . .

- **RUSH TO FINALIZE THE LAYOUT**. Itemizing everything first is how you will create an efficient space that can grow with you.
- **IGNORE THE PRODUCTS THAT KEEP YOU ORGANIZED**. Cut corners here, and it bleeds into everything else.
- **OVERLOOK THE WALL AS ANOTHER STORAGE SOLUTION**. You can mount so many things on it, from the vacuum cleaner to your ironing board.

Half laundry room, half mudroom, this beautiful hallway in my design partner Lauren's home is hiding a stacked washer and dryer, and a storage framework that houses everything from cleaning supplies to children's sneakers behind closed doors.

CREATING A CUSTOM LAUNDRY ROOM

There is something wonderful that happens in the home when there is a place to neatly house all the things that keep it running (light bulbs, batteries, extra tape) and the people in it happy and healthy.

The process for designing a laundry room is similar to laying out a closet: Consider function first. Take inventory of what needs to be kept in the space. Measure everything. When I am mapping out a laundry room, I also take the client's task list into account. What do they want to achieve in this space: ironing, handwashing, line drying? Then I look at what built-ins I can add to make those chores easier. These pages include a few of my go-to tools for getting the job done efficiently.

1. **INSTALL A HANGING ROD.** You'll use it for everything from air-drying clothes to sorting pieces before they are hung in the closet.
2. **INVEST IN A PULL-OUT FOLDING STATION** if you aren't able to include a counter. The extra surface helps speed up everything.
3. **A CADDY IS IMPERATIVE.** Having all the detergent, fabric softeners, and stain removers in one, easy-to-access spot is a game changer.
4. **VINTAGE EVEN HERE!** We use this brass Italian wall rack from the 1960s, which I found on LiveAuctioneers, for air-drying clothes and to hang pieces while they are being steamed.

ANOTHER THING . . .

If you are updating a kitchen, consider taking on the laundry room, too. There is a lot of material overlap between the two spaces, and it is often more affordable to add a few extra cabinets for your laundry room to a larger kitchen order than it is to purchase them in small amounts.

ORGANIZING A LAUNDRY ROOM WITH

JULIA PINSKY

THREE STEPS TO GETTING STARTED

STEP 1: DEFINE WHAT BELONGS IN THIS ROOM AND WHAT DOES NOT. People often use their laundry room as a catchall for everything they don't know what to do with, which leads to chaos. I suggest sticking to the following: laundry supplies; cleaning products and equipment; first aid kits and medicine; and household supplies, like batteries, light bulbs, or the paper products you bought in bulk.

STEP 2: SEPARATE YOUR LAUNDRY ROOM INTO ZONES. Group items according to the categories you defined in step one. Then plan your space based on storage needs: drawers versus shelves, for instance. Try to house all of the items from each category in the same area.

STEP 3: LABEL EVERYTHING—shelves, drawers, and the individual dividers within each of those spaces. It is a time-consuming but essential step to keep things organized in the long run.

HELPFUL TIPS FOR ORGANIZING LAUNDRY SUPPLIES

YOU CAN'T KEEP EVERYTHING. It's okay to toss the lone sock that's been sitting on your dryer for a month. Its friend isn't coming back.

DECANT LAUNDRY DETERGENT into a pretty container.

THERE ARE A HUNDRED WAYS TO USE A LAZY SUSAN: as a button lost and found; as a place to keep stain removers and lint rollers; as a catchall for clothes pins, dryer balls, and other small essentials.

HELPFUL TIPS FOR ORGANIZING CLEANING AND FIRST AID SUPPLIES

KEEP FIRST AID SUPPLIES IN A DRAWER or their own kit for emergencies. I have one in the laundry room and another in the kitchen.

STORE MEDICATION IN LABELED DRAWERS THAT LOCK. Separate them into medicine, supplements, and vitamins, and put each into a small acrylic bin within the drawer.

STORE CLEANING SUPPLIES IN PLASTIC BINS before putting them in a cabinet or on a shelf. These bottles often leak; washable containers will make your life easier.

SHALLOW STORAGE IS A GOOD IDEA. Shelves with a depth of four to five inches mean you can line up cleaning products and extra toiletries in a single, neat row.

DEDICATE A DRAWER FOR REFILLS: Extra Swiffer pads, microfiber cleaning cloths, vacuum attachments, etc.

MAKE SAFETY A PRIORITY. Toxic cleaning products belong in a clearly labeled container on a high shelf where children can't reach them.

PROJECT LIGHT BULB

Can good organization solve your most annoying housekeeping tasks? The answer is yes. When we lived in Los Angeles, our home had what felt like a hundred different light fixtures, each with its own specific bulb. When one would burn out, I would spend hours searching for the correct replacement. One afternoon, I took every light bulb in the house, sorted them by wattage, and labeled which fixture they belonged to.

This is Project Light Bulb 2.0. I used the same sorting system from our LA home in our NYC townhouse, which has far fewer light fixtures, but the level of organization makes me happy.

ABOVE: Our NYC laundry room has a wall of shallow storage on the right, floating shelves, and a vintage hanging rack (which you can see on page 351). The simple framework brings functionality to this space—and, more importantly, my life. It is not necessarily the most expensive upgrades that make the difference; it is choosing the *right* ones.

OPPOSITE: A single bank of cabinets fits everything this 64-square-foot space needs to function: a compartment for mops and brooms, a counter for laundry soap, and enough closed storage for all the cleaning supplies.

LG

LET'S TALK ABOUT MUDROOMS

Dedicating square footage to creating a mudroom is a reach-for moment that is worth the stretch. This space can give you back the thirty minutes you spend hanging up coats and putting away shoes after your kids are asleep. Assign each family member a zone that includes a place for their shoes, coats, bags, sporting equipment, etc. When things have a designated home, it becomes instinct to put them away.

You don't have to have a "room" to create a mudroom; a space at the end of the hall, a closet under the stairs, even a corner of the garage can be used for this purpose. You only need 24 inches of depth to build a cabinet to hang coats. Ideally, the space you find is close to where you enter the home. If that is not an option, carving out an area a bit further away from the front door should not be a dealbreaker.

1. **DESIGNATE A MAILROOM.** In our home, we have a closet specifically for packages. As a result of what Jeremiah and I do, our deliveries could rival a small-town post office. In this Chicago mudroom, we left an open shelf inside a back cabinet for incoming boxes and mail.

2. **INCLUDE SPACE FOR YOUR FUR FAMILY**. Start with the essentials: a place for them to eat, a drawer for all their belongings, and a hook for leashes. Then you can think about whether you need high-end upgrades, like built-in beds or self-filling water bowls.

3. **SHOE STORAGE SHOULD BE EASY FOR EVERYONE**. For a project in Minneapolis we designed cabinetry with deep bottom drawers for shoes. The fronts have brass grilles for ventilation, because, well, kids' sneakers.

2

1

3

WHERE HARDWORKING MEETS HANDSOME

In a room dedicated to hiding things away, make what you see count. Choose a deep paint color for the walls or millwork. Consider a wallcovering that introduces some texture. I like pattern on the floor, a checked tile or striped runner—as long as it is easy to clean. Doing something innovative and unexpected is worth the time and creativity.

DO YOU HAVE ROOM FOR . . .

1. **A CHEST OF DRAWERS?** Furniture creates contrast in a space full of millwork. The extra surface allows you to add personal objects, like framed photos or handsome bowls for keys.

2. **A BENCH?** A place to sit and take off your shoes is less chaotic all around, especially when you have young kids. If you need more storage, a row of baskets can go underneath.

3. **A SINK?** Having a utility sink is great for washing out mops, gardening projects, or bathing a pet—things you'd rather *not* do at your kitchen sink.

1

2

3

PANTRIES

Whether you have one that you walk into or kitchen cabinets that hold food, a pantry is about one thing: organization. This high-traffic area can easily get away from you. A single unsupervised snack time in our home and chaos sets in. Take the time to put the right tools in place and develop a labeling system—see page 364 for advice on both. Here are more ideas to help you start the organizing process:

- Find and follow the experts, including Julia Pinksy (@pinskyproject), Brandie Larsen and Ryan Eisland (@homesort), and Nialya Suarez (@organized_simplicity).
- Invest in quality storage solutions. Buy it once, and you live well forever.
- Pay attention to ventilation. A space that is cool with good airflow is ideal.
- Add some counter space, which you will use more often than you think. If you like to entertain, it's where the dishes land until the party is over.

Lauren loves to cook and entertain, so she created a pantry for food and a separate butler's pantry (seen here), which houses the overflow from her kitchen: specialty cookware, an extra coffee machine, and everything she needs to feed her dog.

WHATEVER YOU DO, PLEASE DON'T . . .

- **PILE THINGS FRONT TO BACK ON DEEP SHELVES.** You will be constantly searching for what you need—and knocking everything else over in the process.
- **KEEP EXPIRED FOOD IN THE HOUSE.** Pick a day. Mark your calendar. Check the use-by dates.
- **PANIC IF YOU DON'T HAVE AN INSTAGRAM-WORTHY PANTRY**, or even a designated pantry at all. Perfection is not the goal; a system that functions for you is.

For a project in Lake Forest, Illinois, we included a combination of closed and open storage. There is a wall of cabinetry as you enter the room, and floating shelves on the back wall.

BAKING
SUGAR
DARK BROWN SUGAR
CANDY
RUMMO
ISOLA
ITALIAN TOMATOES
PEELED
VEGAN REFRIED PINTO BEANS
PASTA & RICE
YELLOWFIN TUNA
GENOVA

ORGANIZING A PANTRY WITH

JULIA PINSKY

THREE STEPS TO GETTING STARTED

STEP 1: ASSESS THE SITUATION. Most people expect too much from their pantry. It is for storing food first, and large cookware, if you have the space. Everything else—cleaning products, medicine, overflow household items—should be moved to another room.

STEP 2: SORT FOOD BY CATEGORIES. This will form the foundation of your storage plan. Divide items by type: pasta, grains, salty snacks, sweet snacks, etc.

STEP 3: PLAN YOUR STORAGE. Each category should have its own shelf or a clearly defined section of a shelf. Keep the most-used items at eye level, cookware on higher shelves, and, if you have kids, their snacks go on a shelf that's low enough for them to reach.

OTHER CONSIDERATIONS

INVOLVE AN ORGANIZER, IF YOU CAN. Hiring a professional is the best way to ensure an efficient pantry layout. This is a space that, despite its typically small footprint, is a big undertaking.

DECANT WHAT YOU CAN. It makes your pantry nicer to look at and the things in it easier to find. I like to use glass or acrylic jars with plastic, wooden, or bamboo lids.

INVEST IN A LAZY SUSAN, so you don't have to store things front to back. They are great for kids' snacks, protein bars, tea bags, etc.

LABEL EVERYTHING. Clear containers lined up on shelves will keep your pantry organized. I use a Cricut label maker, which has a lot of customization options.

CREATE A SPICE DRAWER. Invest in labeled, uniform containers. File your spices alphabetically or by frequency of use, with the ones you need most often at the front of the drawer.

EVERYTHING HAS ITS PLACE, EVEN IN THE FRIDGE. Condiments go in the door, ready-to-eat food at eye level, meat on lower shelves, and fruits and vegetables in the drawers. Use clear, labeled, stackable containers for things like berries and cheese.

WHEN FURNITURE SOLVES THE PROBLEM

I have moved homes a lot, including a dozen times since Jeremiah and I have been together. Of all the places I have lived, only two had a designated pantry. What it taught me is that you don't need a walk-in pantry to create a system that works well. Certain cabinets and drawers in the kitchen used only for food storage, or even bringing in a chest of drawers or an armoire can provide the space you need. Here are a few things to keep in mind, if you're piecing together your own framework:

- The organizing rules on page 364 still apply.
- Avoid the urge to buy in bulk, unless you have a separate area for keeping the overflow.
- Plan zones carefully: Snack drawers should be low and accessible. Grains and baking supplies in an upper cabinet close to the stove.
- It is okay to spread storage throughout the kitchen, instead of all in one place, if that's what works best for you.
- If you are renovating your kitchen, consider adding a series of shallow drawers, around 4 inches high. This size is great for spices, silverware, and coffee and tea supplies.

A beautiful piece of old furniture reconfigured to work as a pantry adds history and character in a room full of new cabinetry.

10

THE NUMBERS GAME

11

THE MATERIALS LIBRARY

PART 3

THE DESIGNER'S TOOLBOX

Truly great design comes down to the details. The distance between a side table and a chair, understanding the best height to mount a sconce, or which moulding style will highlight your home's architecture. It has taken me three decades to form a solid foundation of confidence. Learning how to get these components right is the result of countless rounds of trial and error. The chapters that follow are a crash course in fundamentals: the measurements you should know, the projects I would recommend leaving to the pros, and my favorite resources for everything from door knobs to bathroom fixtures.

At my firm, when a project is underway and decisions have been made, we keep physical representations of the material choices stored in a tray. You would be surprised how often you need to reference the color of the wood floor when designing the rest of a room.

It's important to know the rules, but it's not essential to follow them. The average height for a sconce by a fireplace is 6 feet from the floor. If that feels off, try it higher or lower by a few inches. Trust your eye.

10

THE NUMBERS GAME

You are going to need a measuring tape.

MEASUREMENTS TO KNOW

FURNITURE STANDARDS

Sofa: 84 to 96 inches wide, 36 to 42 inches deep, 28 to 38 inches high

Occasional chair: 32 to 40 inches wide, 32 to 40 inches deep, 24 to 36 inches high

Loveseat: 72 inches wide, 36 to 42 inches deep, 28 to 38 inches high

Chaise: 36 to 42 inches wide, 60 to 74 inches deep, 28 to 36 inches high

Dining chair: 21 to 24 inches deep, seat height of 16 to 18 inches, total height of 32 to 36 inches

Coffee table: 42 to 60 inches wide, 18 to 30 inches deep, 12 to 18 inches high

Square side table: 22 to 28 inches wide by 22 to 28 inches deep, 24 to 28 inches high

Round side table: 12 to 21 inches in diameter, 24 to 28 inches high

Console table: 48 to 84 inches wide, 12 to 18 inches deep, 28 to 30 inches high

Armoire: 42 to 52 inches wide, 30 to 36 inches deep, 60 to 90 inches high

Desk: 48 to 72 inches wide, 24 to 36 inches deep, 29 to 30 inches high

Bedside Table: 18 to 36 inches wide, 18 to 21 inches deep, 25 to 28 inches high

Bookcase: 42 to 60 inches wide, 14 to 18 inches deep, 42 to 96 inches high

UPHOLSTERED FURNITURE STANDARDS

Typical seat depth: 24 inches minimum

Typical seat height: 16 to 18 inches

Typical back height: 27 to 30 inches

WINDOW TREATMENTS

Distance between a drapery rod and the ceiling or the bottom of the crown moulding: 3 inches

Distance between the bottom of the drapery and the floor: nothing; it should "kiss" the floor or slightly puddle.

Drapery rods should extend 18 to 20 inches beyond your window casing on either side of the window.

LIGHTING

Distance between the countertop and the bottom edge of a pendant: 36 inches

Distance between the top of your kitchen table and the bottom of a pendant: 30 inches

Clearance under a pendant: 7.5 feet from the floor to the bottom of the fixture.

Typical sconce height: 5.5 feet from the floor to the center of the fixture.

Sconce height by a fireplace: 6 feet from the floor to the center of the fixture.

KITCHEN STANDARDS

Wall-mounted upper cabinet depth: 12 inches

Wall-mounted upper cabinet height: 30 to 48 inches

Distance between the countertop and the bottom of a wall-mounted upper cabinet: 18 inches

Base cabinet depth: 24 inches

Base cabinet height: 34.5 inches (36 inches if you have a 1.5 inch-thick countertop)

Maximum cabinet door width: 24 inches

Countertop height: 36 inches

Bar countertop height: 42 inches

Countertop depth: 24 to 25 inches

Height of counter stool for a 36-inch-high countertop: 24 to 26 inches

Minimum countertop overhang to accomodate counter stool: 10 to 12 inches

Kitchen sink: 30 to 36 inches wide by 20 to 22 inches deep, 8 to 10 inches high

Recommended amount of workspace between the sink and the oven if they are across from each other: 36 to 48 inches

Minimum distance between the kitchen island and perimeter cabinets: 42 inches

Minimum amount of workspace on either side of the range: 12 to 18 inches

BATHROOM STANDARDS

Classic vanity height: 34.5 inches (inclusive of the countertop)

Modern vanity height: 36 inches (inclusive of the countertop)

Vanity countertop dimensions: 24 to 60 inches wide, 21 inches deep

Minimum amount of unobstructed floor space in front of a sink: 36 inches

Bathtub: 60 to 72 inches long, 30 to 36 inches wide, 14 to 17 inches deep

Spa or soaking tub: 66 to 72 inches long, 36 to 40 inches wide, 24 inches deep

Walk-in shower, minimum dimensions: 32 inches wide by 32 inches deep

Height between the shower curtain rod and the floor: 75 to 77 inches

Shower curtain length: 72 inches

Distance between the bottom of the shower curtain and the floor: 3 to 5 inches

Toilet: 30 inches high, 29 inches deep, 18 inches wide

Distance between the toilet roll holder and the floor: 26 to 28 inches

Distance between the towel bar and the floor: 42 to 48 inches

Distance between the top of a towel ring and the floor: 48 to 52 inches

Distance between a robe hook and the floor: 65 to 70 inches

ENTRY STANDARDS

Minimum width of a foyer: 42 inches

Minimum clearance in front of a door, so it can swing open without obstruction: 36 inches

Decorative mirror height: The center should be at eye level or 62 inches off the floor.

Coat closet: a minimum of 36 inches wide by 24 inches deep. Allow 4 to 6 inches of rod width and 18 inches of depth for each coat.

DINING AREA STANDARDS

Dining table height: 29 to 30 inches

Minimum clearance under your dining table: 27 inches

Minimum distance between the seat of your dining chair and the surface of the dining table: 11 to 12 inches

Minimum clearance between the back of a dining chair and the wall (or other furniture) behind it: 36 inches

Space allowance per table setting (to include plate, cutlery, and glassware): 24 inches wide by 15 inches deep

MEASUREMENTS TO KNOW

MINIMUM DIAMETER FOR A ROUND DINING TABLE

To seat four:
42 to 48 inches

To seat six: 54 inches

To seat eight: 72 inches

MINIMUM DIMENSIONS FOR A SQUARE DINING TABLE

To seat two:
24 inches wide by
24 inches deep

To seat four:
36 inches wide by
36 inches deep

To seat eight:
48 inches wide by
48 inches deep

MINIMUM DIMENSIONS FOR A RECTANGULAR DINING TABLE

To seat two:
40 inches wide by
36 inches deep

To seat four:
48 inches wide by
36 inches deep

To seat eight:
78 inches wide by
36 inches deep

LIVING ROOM STANDARDS

Coffee table height: 1 to 2 inches lower than the seat of the sofa.

Footstool and ottoman height: 1 inch lower than the seat of the sofa.

Distance between the front of the sofa and the coffee table: 16 to 18 inches

Distance between the TV and your viewing position: 2.5 to 3 times the vertical height of your television. For example: if you have a 55-inch TV, you should be sitting 11.5 feet away.

Minimum clearance required for pathways moving through the room: 36 inches

Minimum bookcase depth for standard-size books: 10 inches

Minimum bookcase depth for art or coffee table books: 18 inches

STANDARD RUG DIMENSIONS

3 x 5 feet

4 x 6 feet

7 x 9 feet

8 x 10 feet

9 x 12 feet

10 x 12 feet

BEDROOM STANDARDS

Minimum clearance around the bed: 36 inches. For wheelchair access, create enough space for a 5-foot turning circle near the bed.

Bedside table height: plus or minus 3 inches from the top of your mattress.

Wall-mounted reading light: 2 to 6 inches to the side of the headboard, 60 inches above the floor (assuming the top of your mattress is around 24 inches from the floor).

STANDARD MATTRESS SIZES

Crib: 28 inches wide by
53 inches deep

Twin: 38 inches wide by
75 inches deep

Full: 53 inches wide by
75 inches deep

Queen: 60 inches wide by
80 inches deep

King: 76 inches wide by
80 inches deep

California King:
72 inches wide by
84 inches deep

HOME OFFICE STANDARDS

Desk height:
29 to 30 inches

Standing desk height:
36 inches

Desk depth:
24 to 36 inches

Desk chair seat height:
17 to 18 inches

Drawer dimensions to store files laterally:
30, 36, or 42 inches wide by 18 to 20 inches deep, 12 inches high

Drawer dimensions to store files vertically:
18 inches wide by
24 to 28 inches deep,
12 inches high

Drawer height for small office supplies (pencils, paperclips, etc.): 4 to 6 inches

Drawer height for medium-size office supplies (calculator, notebooks, measuring tape): 6 inches

LAUNDRY ROOM STANDARDS

Width of washer and dryer when placed side by side: 60 inches

Minimum depth required for a washer and dryer: 33 inches, plus 6 inches for hoses and venting.

Recommended counter space on at least one side of the washer and dryer: 18 to 36 inches wide, 24 to 25 inches deep

Vertical clearance required for a stacked washer and dryer: 70 to 80 inches from the floor

Clearance required in front of a front-loading washer and dryer: 48 inches

Minimum width for a laundry room entrance: 32 inches to accommodate appliance installation.

CLOSET STANDARDS

Typical closet depth: minimum 24 inches

Single hanging rod height: 65 to 68 inches from the floor; 72 inches for longer garments.

Heights for double hanging rods: 42 inches from the floor for the lower rod; 84 inches for the upper rod.

Drawer depth for folded clothing: minimum 18 to 24 inches

Walk-in closet: minimum 6.5 feet wide by 6.5 feet deep

GENERAL CLOTHING/ SHOE STORAGE MEASUREMENTS

T-shirts: 19 hangers per foot

Jackets and suits: 15 hangers per foot

Simple shirts or dresses: 15 to 16 hangers per foot

Shoe storage: 12 inches wide, 12 inches deep, 4 inches high per pair

Boot storage: 13 inches wide, 13 inches deep, 18 inches high per pair

PANTRY STANDARDS

Reach-in pantries: 5 feet wide by 2 feet deep (on average)

Walk-in pantries: 5 feet wide by 5 feet deep (on average)

GENERAL SHELF MEASUREMENTS

Shelves: 12 to 18 inches deep with 18 to 24 inches of vertical height between each shelf.

Shelves for canned goods: minimum 6 inches deep with 6.5 to 7 inches of vertical height between each shelf.

Shelves for cereal boxes: 14 to 16 inches of vertical height between each shelf.

Shelves for large items such as bins of produce: 18 to 20 inches apart

Leave 2 inches of space above your tallest items to allow sliding things in and out with ease.

MEASURENTS TO TAKE

WHAT TO MEASURE IN EVERY ROOM

Overall dimensions: length, width, and height; note architectural details and their locations.

Walls: length, width, and height; height of baseboard and crown moulding; depth of baseboard and shoe moulding (i.e. the small piece of moulding between the baseboard and the floor); note location of light fixtures and vents.

Ceiling: length and width; note location of light fixtures and vents.

Floor: length and width; note location of vents.

Windows: width, height, and depth; width of window casing.

Doors: width, height, and depth; width of door casing; note location of hinges and direction of door swing.

Door clearances: distance between the top of the door and the ceiling; distance between the bottom of the door and the floor. Open doors to measure clearance in front.

Electrical: note location of wall switches, thermostats, junction boxes, and electrical outlets and panels.

Furniture: height, width, and depth; note placement within the room.

Rugs: height, width, and depth; note placement within the room.

IN THE BATHROOM/ POWDER ROOM

Vanity: height, width, and depth; storage dimensions inside the vanity.

Sink: width, depth, and height; note its location on the countertop.

Faucet: height; note the plumbing configuration (top mount or wall mount) and the number of holes (one, two, or three).

Shower entrance: width, height, and direction of door swing (if applicable).

Toilet: width, depth, and height; round or elongated seat.

IN THE KITCHEN

Upper and lower cabinetry: height, width, and depth; note location within the room.

Drawers: height, width, and depth for drawer inserts.

Counter and island: height, width, and depth; note countertop height and thickness.

Sink: height, width, and depth.

Faucet: Height; note the plumbing configuration (top mount or wall mount) and the number of holes (one, two, or three).

Built-in appliances (range hood, stove, refrigerator, microwave): height, width, and depth; note location within the room.

IN THE ENTRY

Coat closet: height, width, and depth; note location within the room.

IN THE LIVING ROOM/FAMILY ROOM

Distance between the television and your seating configuration.

Fireplace: height, width, and depth; firebox height, width, and depth; note location within the room.

IN THE BEDROOM

Clearance around the larger pieces of furniture: the space between the edge of the bed and the wall, or the side table and the doorframe.

IN THE DINING AREA

Clearance around the dining table with the chairs tucked in and with the chairs pulled out.

What's the largest number of people who fit comfortably around the table?

Tabletop dimensions for seating and centerpiece planning.

In-room storage: height, width, depth, and location of any shelving or drawers.

IN THE OFFICE

In-room storage: height, width, and depth; note location of any built-ins, shelving, or drawers.

IN THE PANTRY

Cabinetry and shelving: height, width, depth, and configuration; note placement within the room.

Drawers: height, width, and depth for organizational inserts.

IN THE LAUNDRY ROOM

Cabinetry and shelving: height, width, depth, and configuration; note placement within the room.

Drawers: height, width, and depth for storage.

Clearance between the wall and the washer and dryer with the doors open, if you have front-loading machines.

IN THE MUDROOM

Cabinetry and shelving: height, width, depth, and configuration; note placement within the room.

Drawers: height, width, and depth for storage.

Amount of open floor space for moving through the room.

REALITY CHECK

BETTER LEAVE IT TO THE PROS

There are certain projects I always call a professional to handle: if a job must be done to code; if the risk of hurting yourself is high; if you're installing or working with particularly expensive materials. The money you are trying to save by taking on the job yourself is not worth the risk of what it could cost if it all went wrong. These are the tasks I recommend leaving to the experts:

- Anything electrical (with the exception of swapping outlet or switch plate covers).
- Anything involving plumbing is never a simple undertaking.
- Connecting something to a gas line (appliances, fireplaces, or lighting).
- Mold abatement.
- Installing major appliances, windows, or doors.
- Masonry work (including fireplaces).
- Intricate tile work.
- Installing stone countertops (which can crack easily).
- Covering a wall with antique mirrored panels, which requires an expert glass cutter.
- Hanging wallpaper with an intricate pattern or repeat.
- Finishing drywall.
- Painting walls that are in terrible condition.

Beautifully aged hardware and moulding, both original to the nineteenth-century home.

11

THE MATERIALS LIBRARY

Our most trusted design resources.

THE WALLCOVERINGS

PAINT

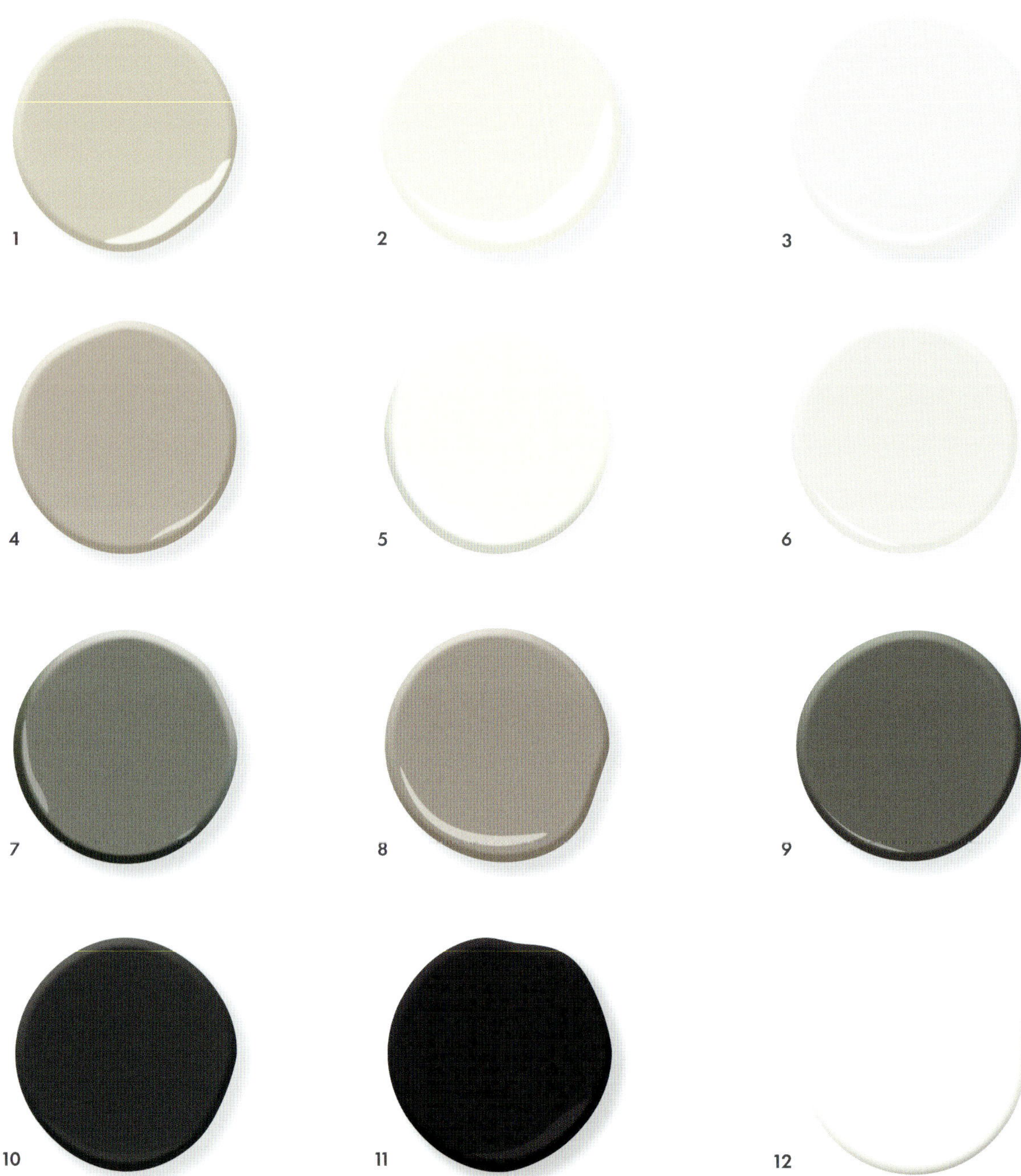

DECODING FINISHES: PAINT

- Ceiling: flat
- Walls: eggshell
- Trim: satin or semi-gloss
- Millwork and doors: Fine Paints of Europe for high gloss (also great for walls in areas you want to stand out, like powder rooms, bars, or studies.)

LIMEWASH

TEXTURED WALLPAPER

1. Shaded White by Farrow & Ball, farrow-ball.com
2. White Dove by Benjamin Moore, benjaminmoore.com
3. Elizabeth I by Portola Paints, portolapaints.com
4. Drop Cloth by Farrow & Ball, farrow-ball.com
5. Snowfall White by Benjamin Moore, benjaminmoore.com
6. Saint Sauvant by Portola Paints, portolapaints.com
7. Card Room Green by Farrow & Ball, farrow-ball.com
8. Smokey Taupe by Benjamin Moore, benjaminmoore.com
9. Nitty Gritty by Portola Paints, portolapaints.com
10. Studio Green by Farrow & Ball, farrow-ball.com
11. Black by Benjamin Moore, benjaminmoore.com
12. Brooks by Portola Paints, portolapaints.com
13. Chemise by Domingue, dominguefinishes.com
14. Carrière by Domingue, dominguefinishes.com
15. Absinthe by Domingue, dominguefinishes.com
16. Terre by Domingue, dominguefinishes.com
17. Sasha by Cannon and Bullock, cannonbullock.com
18. Two-Tone Raffia by Gregorius Pineo, (available in multiple colors), gregoriuspineo.com
19. Hinson Madagascar in Grand by Scalamandre, scalamandre.com
20. Perfect Pair in Toffee by Carlisle & Co., hollyhunt.com

THE DOORS

1. TS1000 Flat Panel Door with Roman Ogee Sticking by TruStile, trustile.com
2. TS2200 Flat Two-Panel Door with Quarter Bead Sticking by TruStile, trustile.com
3. TS3000 Flat Three-Panel Door with Quarter Bead Sticking by TruStile, trustile.com
4. TS2060 Flat Two-Panel Door with Quarter Bead Sticking by TruStile, trustile.com
5. 22526A Knob by Merit, meritmetal.com
6. 472/55 Interior Traditional Knob Latchset by Omnia, omniaindustries.com
7. 7774 Door Lever by Frank Allart, frankallart.com
8. SVB.TS.225DI.L130.HD Complete Lever by Sun Valley Bronze, chicagobrass.com
9. 484-2-2-01-11 Euro Entrance Multipoint Backplate (shown with 484 lever, sold separately) by Merit, meritmetal.com
10. P-225DI Bevel Edge Diamond Passage Plate by Sun Valley Bronze, sunvalleybronze.com
11. BD.5048 Rosette by Baldwin, chicagobrass.com
12. 7821 Rosette Concealed Fix by Frank Allart, frankallart.com

1

2

3

4

KNOBS AND LEVERS

5 6 7 8

BACKPLATES AND ROSETTES

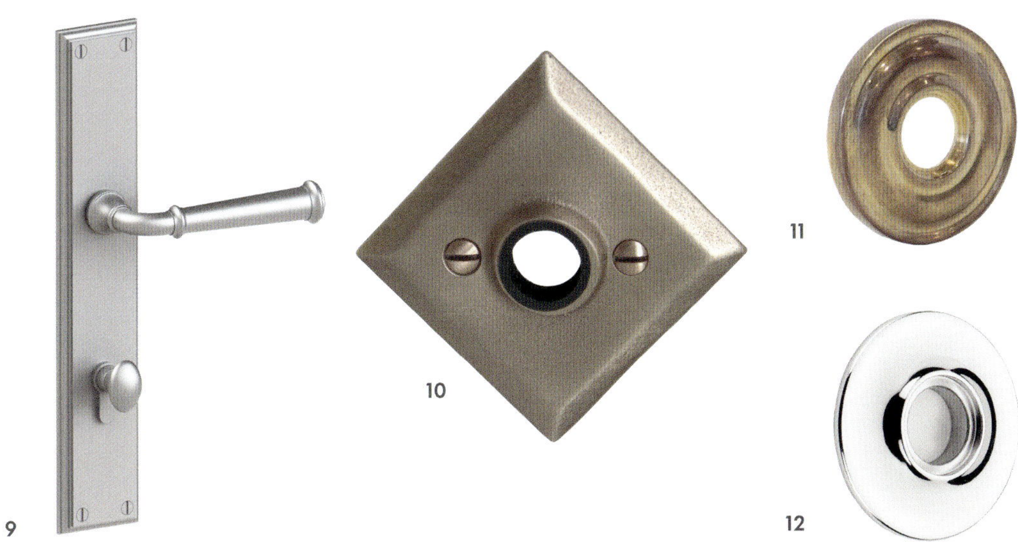

9 10 11 12

THE HARDWARE

1. CS-502/503DB Bevel Edge Auxiliary Deadbolt Set by Sun Valley Bronze, sunvalleybronze.com
2. MM.115.3 Door Stop with Baseboard Mount by Merit Metal, chicagobrass.com
3. SI.5.400605.0 Concealed Adjustable Hinge by SIMONSWERK, chicagobrass.com; (312) 245-0200 to order
4. MM.125BB.239 Two Ball Bearing Hinge with Acorn Finials by Merit, chicagobrass.com; (312) 245-0200 to order
5. Duplex Outlet by Forbes and Lomax in Unlacquered Brass, forbesandlomax.com
6. Switch Plate in Unlacquered Brass by Forbes and Lomax, forbesandlomax.com
7. Custom Bronze Grille by Coco Architectural Grilles & Metalcraft, cocometalcraft.com
8. Laser Cut Aluminum Custom Vent Cover by Pacific Register Company, pacificregister.com
9. C262 Large Curved Bar Handle by Optimum Brasses, optimumbrasses.co.uk
10. Large Bakes Handle by Whitechapel, whitechapel-ltd.com

DOOR BOLTS, STOPS, AND HINGES

1

2

3

4

ELECTRICAL PLATES

5

6

HVAC GRILLES

7

8

APPLIANCE PULLS

9

10

DECODING FINISHES: METAL

- Bronze
- Unlacquered brass
- Polished nickel
- Blackened iron
- Wrought iron

THE CABINET HARDWARE

KNOBS

1

2

3

4

5

6

7

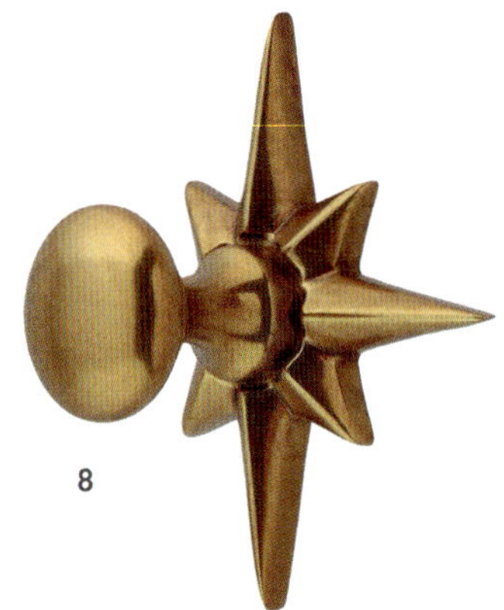
8

9

PULLS AND HANDLES

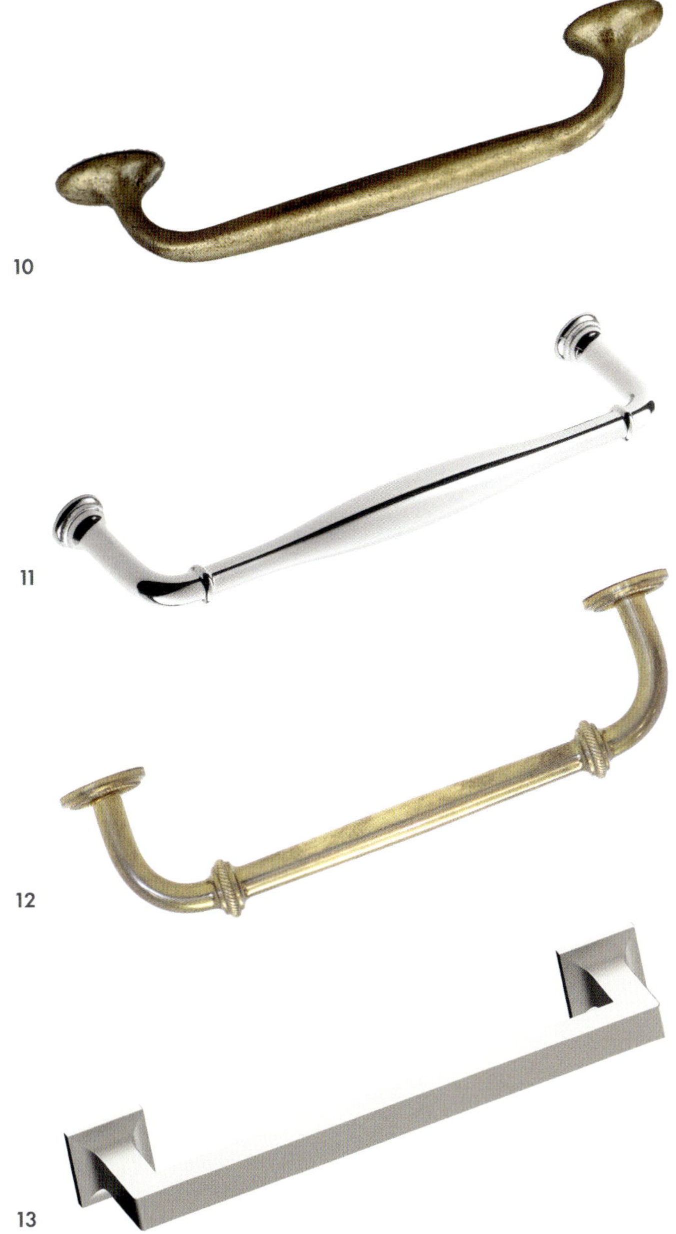
10
11
12
13

HINGES

14

1. Shore 2870 Oval Knob by Classic Brass, classic-brass.com
2. 100KBY15 Plain Cabinet Knob by Whitechapel, whitechapel-ltd.com
3. Hutter 1134 Knob by Classic Brass, classic-brass.com
4. 93KF4 European Cabinet Knob by Whitechapel, whitechapel-ltd.com
5. Chautauqua 3021 Knob by Classic Brass, classic-brass.com
6. 41770 Convex Ring Knob by Merit, alexandermarchant.com
7. Capital Knob by Merit, alexandermarchant.com
8. Polaris Cabinet Knob with Star Back Plate by House of Antique Hardware, houseofantiquehardware.com
9. Egg Cabinet Knob by Rocky Mountain Hardware, rockymountainhardware.com
10. C224 Bar Handle by Optimum Brasses, optimumbrasses.co.uk
11. Chautauqua Pull by Classic Brass, classic-brass.com
12. BDF.PDT-0400.150-MET.ROS-0100-MET Cabinet Pull with Rosettes by Bronzes de France, chicagobrass.com; (312) 245-0200 to order
13. 30102-6 Drawer Pull by Merit, meritmetal.com
14. Solid Brass Olive Knuckle Hinge by Deltana, myknobs.com

THE ARCHITECTURAL MATERIALS

1. Paonazzo Marble by ABC Worldwide Stone, abcworldwidestone.com
2. Nero Marquina Marble by ABC Worldwide Stone, abcworldwidestone.com
3. Arabescato Corchia Marble by ABC Worldwide Stone, abcworldwidestone.com
4. Calacatta Viola Marble by ABC Worldwide Stone, abcworldwidestone.com
5. Reclaimed Petit Granite by Exquisite Surfaces, xsurfaces.com
6. Hand Antiqued Blond Sancerre Limestone by Paris Ceramics, parisceramicsusa.com
7. Honed Spanish Dark Grey Marble and Honed Spanish Superior White Marble by Paris Ceramics, parisceramicsusa.com
8. Honed Belgium Blue Limestone by Paris Ceramics, parisceramicsusa.com. Where to use it: An entryway or office floor.
9. Reclaimed Square Terracotta Tiles by Exquisite Surfaces, xsurfaces.com
10. Bordeaux Black Herringbone Limestone Tile by François & Co, francoisandco.com
11. Black/Ebony Penny Round Keystones by Daltile, daltile.com. How to use it: Mix with Arctic White Penny Round Keystones to make a striped shower floor.
12. Arctic White Penny Round Keystones by Daltile, daltile.com
13. Sheer White Oak by The Hudson Company, thehudsonco.com
14. Normandie Natural French Oak by Exquisite Surfaces, xsurfaces.com
15. Patina Walnut Antique by LV Wood, lvwood.com

MARBLE

1

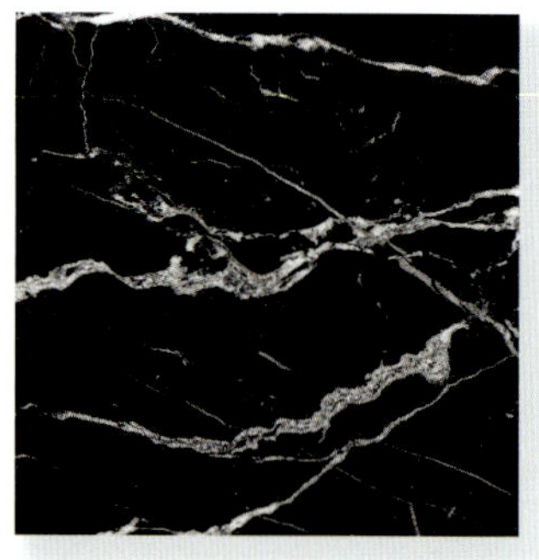
2

3

4

STONE FLOORS

5

6

TILE FLOORS

7

8

9

10

11

12

WOOD FLOORS

13

14

15

THE FIREPLACES

MANTELS

1

2

3

4

FIREBRICKS

5

6

THE WINDOW TREATMENTS

SHADES

7

8

DRAPERIES

9

10

1. Walden Arabescato by Jamb, jamb.co.uk
2. Argyll by Jamb, jamb.co.uk
3. Jordan by Ancient & Modern, ancientandmodern.us
4. Louis XIV Style Fireplace in Rance Marble Circa 1888 from Frédéric Dulyère, 1stdibs.com
5. Antique Briquettes Firebricks by François & Co., francoisandco.com
6. Herringbone Firebrick in Ochre by Exquisite Surfaces, xsurfaces.com
7. Relaxed Roman Shade by The Shade Store, theshadestore.com
8. Flat Roman Shade by The Shade Store, theshadestore.com
9. Pinch Pleat Drapery by The Shade Store, theshadestore.com
10. Ripple Fold Drapery by The Shade Store, theshadestore.com

THE BATHROOM FITTINGS

SINKS

1

2

3

4

TOILETS

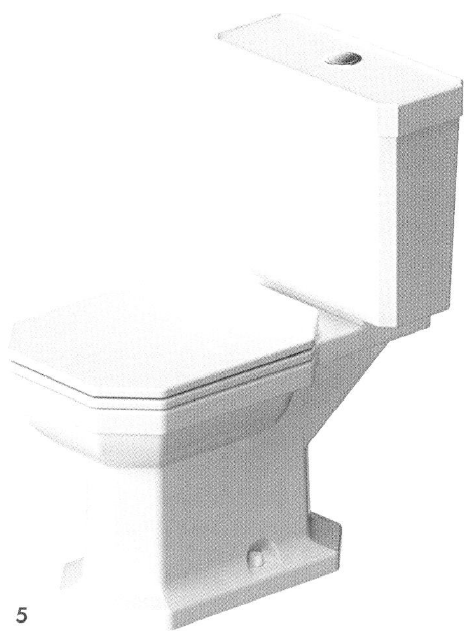

5

6

1. Henry Metal Round Single Two-Leg Washstand by Waterworks, waterworks.com
2. Washstand Base with Skirted Straight Legs by Urban Archaeology, urbanarchaeology.com
3. Soho Basin by the Water Monopoly, thewatermonopoly.com. (Pedastal sold separately.)
4. 1930 Wall-Mounted Sink by Duravit, duravit.us
5. 1930 Two-Piece Toilet by Duravit, duravit.us
6. Westminster Wall-hung W.C. Pan by Devon & Devon, devon-devon.com

ACKNOWLEDGMENTS

The thirty years of design experience reflected in these pages would not be possible without the trust of the many clients we have had the great privilege of creating spaces for. Thank you for opening your doors.

To the incredible force of joy and experience that is Jan Miller: Why do it if you aren't going to laugh hysterically the whole time?

Thank you, Ali Kominsky at Dupree Miller, for your unwavering enthusiasm and support.

To dearest Doris Cooper, who was renovating her own apartment while editing this book; I've always wanted to work with you from the day we met over twenty-five years ago. I'm so thrilled I finally had the opportunity, and it went exactly as I knew it would. You are brilliant, kind, and don't miss a thing. Thank you for loving this idea, for every note, and for every comment in the margins.

To the incredible team at Simon Element, Richard Rhorer, Maria Espinosa, Jen Wang (who cracked the cover design in one pass), Alyssa diPierro, Jessica Preeg, Laura Jarrett, Allison Har-zvi, and Jessie McNiel: What a talented, creative, dedicated, and brilliant group of people. Don't even try to do a book without them.

To all of the photographers, stylists, and visual teams whose beautiful work appears in this book, I thank you.

I have nothing but gratitude for the experts who agreed to be featured in *Foundations*. I set out to include the people I most admire, and I thank you all for lending your perspectives and advice:

Aerin Lauder: Who may be the most elegant and charming person to exist.

Stephen Fanuka: Whose flawless construction I have come to depend on.

Mary Jeanne Kneen: Whose elevated eye has taught me so much over the years.

Julia Pinsky: Your level of organization is borderline pornographic to me.

Marlene Poynder and the team at The Carlyle: Who better to ask how to make guests feel at home?

To Krista Blair, Phoebe Craig, and the teams at Nate Berkus Associates in Chicago, New York City, and Los Angeles, I hope you know how valued you are every day; it's one of my greatest joys to work beside all of you and witness your talent in action.

To Lauren Buxbaum Gordon: You are family to me, which will make more sense when I move into your beautiful home. Thank you for the melted ice cream cone a million years ago and everything that you've done since, and for letting your home illustrate what is magical about design in this book.

To Kelly Engstrom, you pulled off the behind-the-scenes of this entire book flawlessly and with so much passion from day one, just like you do with everything, every day. Thank you for every photo shoot, every five-hour Zoom, every single thing. Please never leave, but if you decided to study magic, I would support you as you definitely pulled a rabbit out of a hat with this one.

To Meredith Smerchek, how is it possible that I keep asking you to do more, and you haven't lost your mind, and you still are the most fun to be around? Your talent, your eye, your instincts are incredible; you are also everyone's favorite person. I am so very lucky to have had you in my corner all of these years. You really out did yourself with the design of this book.

To Heather Summerville, I've said it a thousand times out loud . . . what would I have done without you? I'm so terrible at organizing my thoughts, and you are brilliant. I'm so bad at math, and you are brilliant. Your creativity, talent, and dedication are unmatched. Thank you for agreeing to do this book together, for the laughter along the way. Here is to Chanel slingbacks and spa days and parenthood and awful timelines.

To my family, I love you so much. Someday I will slow down, and you can really come for me about my eating habits and how great I am at texting.

FRENCH ESSENCE
VICKI ARCHER
Indian Interiors
LOUIS VUITTON
The Private World of Yves Saint Laurent & Pierre Bergé
PHILLIPS
JAMES BROWN HANDBOOK
A HOUSE IS NOT A HOME Bruce Weber
JULIAN SCHNABEL
LIVE BEAUTIFUL
CASA MEXICO
RAPHAEL
GEORGIA O'KEEFFE
FREDERICK LAW OLMSTED
Wolfgang T
BEAUTY
BEAUTÉ EN VOYAGE
THE WORLD OF MURIEL BRANDOLINI
THE AZTECS
Great Museums of Italy
SERRALVES 1940
MEXICO
Splendors of Thirty Centuries
Sièges africains
A MAN & HIS WATCH
Uncommon Vernacular
ICONS OF MEN'S STYLE
MARGARET BOURKE-WHITE
MEDICI A FIRENZE

CREDITS

Thank you to all the incredibly talented photographers, stylists, artists, and makers whose work is featured in this book.

PHOTOGRAPHY

Jenna Peffley: pages 1, 37 (1), 43 (4), 75 (right), 78, 127 (1), 140 (left), 156–157, 159 (left), 162, 168 (right), 192, 201, 214-215, 227 (3), 229 (4), 232, 233 (5), 235 (3), 238 (right), 244, 245 (3), 246–247, 250–251, 255 (2), 257 (left), 267 (2), 269 (left), 270 (right), 272–273, 317 (5), 346-347, 351 (3), 353 (left)

Kelly Marshall: pages 2, 4–5, 6 (left), 7 (right), 13, 20–21, 25 (4), 29 (right), 37 (2), 40, 49, 68–69, 75 (left), 84 (3), 87, 128–129, 132, 138, 139 (top), 140 (right), 142–143, 145, 150–151, 155 (top), 158 (left + right), 160–161, 165 (4), 166, 173, 178 (1), 187 (2), 188–189 (1), 193, 195 (right), 202-203, 208, 211 (3), 216 (right), 220–221, 226 (2), 227 (4), 239 (right), 257 (right), 262–263, 267 (1), 270 (left), 271 (left), 278–279, 282–283, 286–287, 289, 291 (3), 294, 298–299 (left), 339, 341 (2), 342, 364, 397

Peter Murdock: pages 6 (right), 33 (right), 84 (2), 89 (moulding), 122, 147 (3), 148, 159 (right), 165 (3), 167, 177 (4), 180 (right), 181 (left), 184, 190, 194 (right), 217 (left), 255 (4), 258 (left), 267 (4), 271 (right), 291 (1, 2), 299 (right), 302–303 (1, 3), 317 (4), 320, 323 (right), 341 (1), 345 (left)

Heather Talbert: pages 7 (left), 8–9, 14-15, 25 (2, 3), 31, 34, 37 (3), 43 (1, 2, 3), 46, 50–51, 62–63, 73, 82 (left), 84 (1), 90, 93, 106, 107, 108–109, 114–115, 116–117, 120, 124, 127 (2, 3), 131 (1, 4, 6), 133 (top left, bottom left, bottom right), 134–135, 139 (bottom), 141, 144, 146 (1), 149, 154, 165 (1, 2), 169 (right), 170–171, 177 (1, 3), 178 (2), 179 (3), 181 (right), 185 (top), 186, 187 (3), 189 (2), 191, 194 (left), 196–197, 198–199, 206-207, 209, 211 (2), 212, 213, 217 (right), 218–219, 225, 226 (1), 229 (2, 3), 230–231, 233 (2, 3, 4), 235 (2), 238 (left), 239 (left), 240–241, 242 (right), 243, 245 (2), 248–249, 252-253, 255 (1, 3), 256, 258 (right), 259, 261, 267 (3), 274, 275 (top left), 276–277, 280–281, 285, 288, 296–297, 303 (2), 305 (left), 311 (1, 4), 312–313, 314-315 (center), 316, 317 (2), 318–319, 321, 324 (left), 331, 337, 341 (3), 344 (left), 345 (right), 348–349, 351 (1), 355, 357 (1, 2), 358–359, 360–361, 362–363, 367, 372, 380

Nicole Franzen: pages 11, 18–19, 33 (left), 70, 112–113, 131 (3), 169 (left), 174–175, 200, 228, 234–235 (1), 292–293, 304 (right), 305 (right), 326, 334–335 (1)

Julie Holder: pages 23, 25 (1), 29 (left), 41, 76 (2), 131 (2), 133 (top right), 177(2), 179 (4), 180 (left), 189 (3), 195 (left), 295, 306–307, 314 (left), 315 (right), 351 (2, 4), 352, 353 (right), 354

Christopher Dibble: pages 26–27, 30, 35, 44–45 (bottom), 58–59, 76 (1, 3), 80, 131 (5), 147 (2), 163, 168 (left), 182–183, 185 (bottom), 264–265, 268 (left), 269 (right), 275 (bottom/ sidebar), 304 (left), 311 (2), 317 (3), 322–323 (left), 324 (right), 325 (right), 335 (2, 3), 343 (left), 344 (right)

Gigi DeManio: page 39 (bottom)

Joshua Gaddy for Exante Antiques + Nate Berkus resale / 1stDibs: page 40, 41, 53, 55, 56, 57, 60, 61, 64, 65, 66, 67, 140, 194, 216

Douglas Friedman / Trunk Archive: page 44 (top)

Dan Arnold for Nate Berkus resale / 1stDibs: page 53, 54, 66

Gabby Exner for Nate Berkus resale / 1stDibs: page 54

Spacecrafting: pages 82 (right), 268 (right), 275 (top right), 300–301, 308–309, 325 (left), 357 (3)

Martha Levisman Collection, Di Tella Arquitectura Archive, EAEU, UTDT: page 95

Laurent Moreau / Hemis / Alamy Stock Photo: page 96 (left)

Horst P. Horst, Vogue, © Condé Nast: page 96 (right)

Stephen Kent Johnson / OTTO: page 97 (left)

Francois Halard / Trunk Archive: page 97 (right)

Charles Peed for Casa Gusto: pages 99 (top left, middle left, bottom center, top right), 103 (6)

Billal Taright: page 99 (top center)

Kevin Leitch, Project Five Studios: page 99 (bottom left)

Gentl and Hyers / Il Buco Cookbook: page 99 (bottom right)

Adrian Gaut / Galerie Half: page 103 (1)

Lauren Buxbaum Gordon: page 103 (2)

Noua Unu Studio / Seventh House Gallery: page 103 (3)

Giancarlo Botti / Gamma-Rapho via Getty Images: page 103 (4)

Francesco Lagnese / OTTO: page 103 (5)

Marc McAndrews: pages 118–119, 211 (4)

Nate Berkus Associates Floorplans: pages 121, 123, 125

Pieter Estersohn: page 136

Roger Davies: pages 152, 260, 333

Ashley Burns: page 155 (bottom)

Simon Upton / Interior Archive: pages 204 (tablescape by Aerin Lauder), 311 (3)

Sam Frost: pages 211 (1), 222–223

Thomas Loof / Trunk Archive: page 216 (left)

John Lamparski / WireImage: page 236

Evan Joseph: page 242 (left)

Rich Stapleton: pages 328–329, 330, 332

Miki Duisterhof: page 336

Maxim Smirnov, MXM / Courtesy of Pinsky Project Home Concierge: pages 343, 365

Sydney Jones: pages 370–371

Dennis Gocer / The Collective You: back cover portrait of Nate Berkus

PRODUCTS

Modernisten, Swedish Modern Cabinet: page 56

Cityscape Pendant Light by Robert Sonneman, Decorum Decorative Finds: page 60

Lanterns, Old Plank Antiques: page 61

European Cabinet Knobs by Whitechapel: page 89

Victorian Oak Double Doors, 1stDibs: page 89

Reclaimed Spanish Terracotta Tiles by Exquisite Surfaces: page 89

Louis XIV Style Fireplace in Rance Marble Circa 1888 from Frédéric Dulyère, 1stDibs: page 89

Vintage bronze bird table, 1stDibs: page 106

Willy Guhl "Handkerchief" planter, Etsy: page 106

Vintage Jacques Adnet lounge chairs, Old Plank Antiques: page 106

Biarritz Gilt fabric (on lounge chairs), Rogers & Goffigon: page 106

Vintage René Prou coffee table, 1stDibs: page 106

Lutyens Bolection in Nero Marquina marble, Jamb: page 106

French, 1940s iron and gilt sconces by Raymond Subes, Thomas Brillet: page 106

Vintage tole lantern, Lorfords: page 106

French 1950s ottoman, 1stDibs: page 107

French, nineteenth-century center hall table, Old Plank Antiques: page 107

Custom jute rug, Hinkins & Associates: page 107

Vintage Stilnovo lamp, Pavilion Antiques: page 107

Vintage pottery, Etsy: page 107

Antique French tapestry, Etsy: pages 108–109

Custom sofa, Estudio Furnishings: pages 108–109

Miguel Stracciatella/Liquorice striped fabric (on sofa), C&C Milano: pages 108–109

Eighteenth-century French urns, W. Gardner, Ltd: pages 108–109

Vintage Danish leather armchairs, Lucca Antiques: pages 108–109

Custom coffee table, Old Plank Antiques: pages 108–109

Custom cube side table, Pavilion Antiques: pages 108–109

Vintage Italian, floor lamp, Danke Galerie: pages 108–109

ART

Fernando Bengoechea / Marcelo Bengoechea: pages 38, 39 (top)

Giovanni Stradone, Notturno Antico: page 67

Antonio Ferrer (right): page 103 (1)

Tor Bjurstrom (left): page 103 (1)

Oil on wood panel by Kyohei Inukai (above fireplace): page 106

Antique oil painting (left), J. Garrett Auctioneers / LiveAuctioneers: page 106

Acrylic on handmade paper by Alejo Palacios (right): page 109

Henryk Lobaczewski, Solid State 'Ode to Yves' #3, Tappan: page 166

Thomas Leyland, Cubist Woman, oil on canvas: page 270

An Imprint of Simon & Schuster, LLC
1230 Avenue of the Americas
New York, NY 10020

First Simon Element hardcover edition November 2025

SIMON ELEMENT is a trademark of Simon & Schuster, LLC

Simon & Schuster strongly believes in freedom of expression and stands against censorship in all its forms. For more information, visit BooksBelong.com.

For information about special discounts for bulk purchases, please contact Simon & Schuster Special Sales at 1-866-506-1949 or business@simonandschuster.com.

The Simon & Schuster Speakers Bureau can bring authors to your live event. For more information or to book an event, contact the Simon & Schuster Speakers Bureau at 1-866-248-3049 or visit our website at www.simonspeakers.com.

Book design by Meredith Smerchek, Jan Derevjanik, Jen Wang

Manufactured in Canada

10 9 8 7 6 5 4 3 2

Library of Congress Cataloging-in-Publication Data has been applied for.

ISBN 978-1-6680-2613-7
ISBN 978-1-6680-2614-4 (ebook)